MERCHANTS OF
DEBT
& OTHER ESSAYS

MERCHANTS OF
DEBT
& OTHER ESSAYS

PRAFULL GORADIA

Wit Books

Wit Books and Services Pvt Ltd
2/15, Ansari Road, Daryaganj
New Delhi-110002
info@witbooks.in

ISBN 978-93-90961-82-5
© Prafull Goradia
First Edition 2022

MRP ₹ 595

Edited by Veena Batra
Cover and layout by Somesh Kumar Mishra
Printed by Vikas Computer and Printers

Contents

THE ARC OF PROSPERITY

Merchants of Debt, the Wealth of Nations

The Crash of 2008: How Unregulated Capital Caused It by Arthur Swan, edited and revised by David M Pidcock has three special virtues: One, the timing of its publication so soon after the meltdown began. Two, the experience of the abuse of money over the centuries is catalogued. Three, the wisdom of distinguished economic minds beginning with Adam Smith, on to David Ricardo and including John Maynard Keynes, is recorded in glimpses. The book has little real research or thinking to its credit. There is very little contemporary comment on the current crash or meltdown. Nevertheless, the volume deserves a look in by laymen as distinct from scholars who would know most of what has been said. The author's motive is best quoted in his own words: "My reason for writing this book is to show that inflation and unemployment are brought about by the same causes; the creation and control of the nation's money supply by the private banking system and interest".

A key to understanding The Crash of 2008 and the current meltdown is to realise that there are two different capitalisms: producer capitalism and credit capitalism. The former is based on the farm and the factory while the latter is housed in banks. The former depends on the production of goods and services while the latter on the issue of metal or paper currency and its subsequent circulation. Money should provide the lubricant to facilitate the production of goods and their free flow forward. By being made adequately available, it can also play the role of stimulating demand and thus encouraging greater production. But that is where the role of money and, its custodian, the bank should be limited. Karl Marx offered a way out: 'If all capital were in the hands of the industrial-capitalist there would be no such thing as interest and rate of interest'.

Instead, the banks assume the role of money manufacturers. They multiply finance in order to earn more and more money for themselves. Abraham Lincoln displayed a rare insight when he commented: "The money power preys upon the nation in times of peace and conspires against it in times of adversity. It is more despotic than monarchy, more insolent than autocracy, more selfish than bureaucracy". The cost of minting coins and printing notes is negligible compared to the interest the banks charge. Even the cost of building and running banks in order to make money accessible to everyone in every part of the country is modest. The central or the reserve bank would be well endowed if it charged say 2 percent to commercial banks who in turn could do well by adding another 2 percent for their upkeep. A total of 4 percent is the very maximum needed to provide banking of cash as well as credit to the entire economy.

Farms and factories produce goods steadily from year to year. The seasonal and incidental fluctuations are seldom big enough to cause either a boom or a slump. Even if an unusual shortage were to lead to a sharp spurt in prices of a few items, they would come down with increased supplies before long. So is the case with an unusual oversupply and fail in prices. The rise and fall in prices is neither long-lasting nor does it affect the rest of the economy. The goods-led fluctuations are compartmental just as they are short-lived. The crashes, whether of 2008 or 1929 or the recessions in between covered entire economies and were not confined to any one country. In 1929, the world was not a global village and yet the ripples that began with a sudden crash in share prices on Wall Street, New York, in October grew into waves that kept battering all the world economies for ten years. Little wonder that Canadian-American economist JK Galbraith wrote: "The study of money, above all other fields in economics is the one in which complexity is used to disguise the truth or to evade the truth, not to reveal it".

How are the steady producing farms and factories harassed by radically unsteady fluctuations, often called slumps and booms, from time to time? With them suffer or prosper the people who work these cradles of production. The demand and supply of goods is, broadly speaking, inelastic. Yet, the prices are at times subjected to violent behaviour. The explanation of author Arthur Swan is that the lure of earning more and more interest makes banks create money beyond the need of the economy. They are then continually looking for borrowers. Their hunt is so frantic that not all those who take the loans are sound operators. Nevertheless, the economy looks large, inflated and blooming. All the economic players enjoy the rocketing boom. At some stage, one or more of the unsound operators fumbles and fails. The bubble bursts; until then all including the farm and factories share the high prices. After the burst, they live to suffer the slump for several years, which is why Lord Keynes advised: "By all means, save wealth for a rainy day but not money".

This phenomenon is reflected in the behaviour of banks in recent years. Many a bank executive was given a monthly target of how much money he had to loan out. This meant that he went out of his way in search of borrowers, perhaps some good and some not so sound. His manager also had targets to fulfill and hence he would also encourage his subordinates to somehow find borrowers. According to the practice in Britain, for every deposit of ten pounds, a commercial bank could lend out nine pounds by way of loans. Imagine, therefore, the multiplicative factor in the availability of money to lend out. Economist Geoffrey Crowther summed this up eloquently: "The banker is a merchant of debt, and his assets as well as liabilities consist merely of debts; the whole system is built up of promises to pay erected on a narrow basis of cash".

Most people who were employed whether on the farm, in the factory or the bank prospered. Everyone made hay while the sun shone. But with doubtful borrowers lurking on the horizon, some had to go under sooner or later. That would set off the crash. In the USA this time around, the early flame of the crash was lit by loans given on houses which were sold by builders at exorbitant prices to people with ordinary means. When the buyers could not pay their instalments, trouble began. The productive industry was thus let down by the finance business; producer capitalism was betrayed by credit capitalism.

The history of credit began in ancient Greece but may have operated in some form or another even earlier. However, its inauguration on a grand scale was when the Bank of England was established by a group of businessmen headed by one William Paterson in 1694 AD with the support of the Chancellor of the Exchequer. At the time, Paterson himself was reported to have said, "The Bank of England hath benefit on all monies it creates out of nothing". Being aware of the dangers of printing paper money, Paterson was against false credit arising out of mere paper issues. Therefore, he never swerved from the safe basis of gold and silver to back up all transferable bills.

Paterson's successors were less conservative and used the power to create money out of nothing. In 1720, the South Sea Company, whose Governor was King George I, was inspired by an enterprising spirit to buy up the entire national debt of Britain. The company began paying 100 percent return and its share price soared between January and August. The company exchanged its shares for the annuities issued by the government; the transaction helped to offset the debt. The Directors could not sustain the hoax and in September the share price crashed. Many investors were ruined. By comparison, the recent Satyam scam would appear elementary. In a chapter of 102 pages 'A Chronological Outline of the Misuse of Money', the book *A History of Abuse and Misuse of Money from Plato to NATO and Beyond* traces the history from 2400 BC Sumeria to 1989 AD, when some of the follies of Thatcherism and Reaganomics of letting the national debt rise indefinitely are enumerated.

Economist Adam Smith, the author of *Capitalism*, had seen

the rise of true capitalism based on the savings of individuals being ploughed back into the business and thereby achieving greater levels of production. He stood for free trade. "A trade which is forced by means of bounties and monopolies may be disadvantageous to the country in whose favour it is meant to be established", wrote Adam Smith. In his magnum opus *An Enquiry into the Nature and Causes of the Wealth of Nations*, Smith said that by the use of banker's money, business can build a pyramid of paper instruments that place a demand on real wealth of the nation. What is happening today is no different from what Adam Smith had predicted implicitly referring to a fourth class of people or landlords who "love to reap where they never sowed".

David Ricardo (1772-1823), a successful stock operator-turned-economist, was no less scathing in his criticism of the nuisance of paper money. The Bullion Committee of 1810 had been set up to consider the issues raised by Ricardo. The main findings of the committee were: The value of notes used as a currency depended on the quantity issued. The quantity of notes to be regulated and their value maintained if the notes were convertible into gold. And yet, the Bank of England spokesman told the Committee, "that no creation of credit by the Bank of England against sound assets could have any effects on prices or exchange rates". On this, Walter Bagehot the famous journalist, reacted by saying, "Such comments had become almost classical by their nonsense".

Nevertheless, in the words of former Bank of England Governor, Lord Montagu Norman, "The dogs may bark but the caravan marches on".

Men of War

Masters of Battle is an eminently apt name given to the book by Terry Brighton. The 439-page volume is a lucidly written epic of three heroes, belonging to three different countries but with one quality in common. All three were brilliant tacticians who could lead troops in battle, outwit the enemy and achieve victory again and again. They were, however, generals who could not always understand the war beyond the battle. Any number of battles were won and lost through the six years of World War II in Europe, from September 1939 to May 1945. The first great victory was won on the outskirts of Warsaw in September 1939, the eighth day since the war began, and the last battle was fought and lost by Germany on the morrow of 30 April 1945 in Berlin, when Adolf Hitler committed suicide.

Battles and the cut and thrust they contain can be exciting and glamorous because they have a unity of space, time and action, rather like a short story, in contrast to a novel. World War II was even longer, an epic and, hence, difficult for a lay reader to comprehend all of it together. The Battle of Benghazi, Rommel's first triumph in Africa on 3 April 1941 or the Battle of El Alamein in November 1942, which made General Montgomery famous, are much more exciting to read and write about than the whole war. All these three heroes made their name and fame in battles. We are not sure that Brighton, the author, quite saw his subjects in such a comprehensive perspective. Had he done so he would not have quoted the praise of Montgomery as the greatest living soldier, of Patton as America's best and of Rommel as Germany's Panzer General. The general of the US Army, Douglas MacArthur, who fought and defeated Japan was by far the outstanding American warrior of the war, as was Heinz Guderian, the finest tank commander, who conceived and created the concept of blitzkrieg (lightning warfare). It would be interesting to refer to Sir Basil Liddell-Hart, the "captain who taught generals". He called Rommel the soldier in the sun (*The Other Side of the Hill*, London, 1948). To quote: "His fame was deliberately fostered—not only by his own efforts, but by Hitler's calculated choice. Hitler, recognising the public craving in wartime for glamorous military figures, decided to pick two soldiers (and two only) whom he could safely turn into popular heroes—"one in the sun and one in the snow". Rommel in Africa was to be the sun-hero and Dietl in Finland was to be the snow-hero.

This is not to underestimate the exploits of Field Marshal Erwin Rommel, but to put his achievement in perspective. The same book praises another soldier: "The ablest of all the German generals was probably Field Marshal Erich von Manstein. That was the verdict of most of those with whom I discussed the war, from Rundstedt downwards. He had a superb strategic sense, combined with a greater understanding of mechanised weapons than any of the generals who did not belong to the tank school itself. Yet in contrast to some of the single-track enthusiasts he did not lose the importance of improving alternative weapons and defence. Dwelling regretfully on Manstein's disappearance from the field, Blumentritt said to me: 'He was not only the most brilliant strategist of all our generals, but had a good political sense. A man of that quality was too difficult for Hitler to swallow for long'."

All the three careers are not only distinguished but also colourful. Let us begin with Montgomery, the English favourite of the English author. Posted in November 1938 to command the 8th Division in Haifa in Palestine to put down an Arab rebellion caused by Jewish immigration, Bernard Law Montgomery told his troops that the insurgents must be hunted relentlessly; when engaged in battle they must shoot to kill. This was the surest way to end the war. The rebellion was smashed within three months. It was difficult to find an Arab insurgent to kill, thereafter. He went on to pursue this strategy in the Second World War. On 20 October 1942, Montgomery's artillery guns opened fire on the Germans at El Alamein. Rommel lost this battle because the tank carrying fuel oil was sunk by the Allies. The battle was lost at sea and not on land. The final verdict on Montgomery at El Alamein is given by Rommel: "The British based their planning on exact calculation, which can only be followed if there is complete material superiority. They undertook no operations but relied solely on their artillery and air force".

Montgomery was egoistical and arrogant. He revelled in his fame as the victor of El Alamein. His appearance at St George's

Cathedral for the Sunday evening service where he read the lesson caused quite a stir. In the words of the Field Marshal: "It is a strange experience to find oneself famous and it would be ridiculous to deny that it was rather fun". Insubordination was another characteristic of Montgomery. In the author's words: "His second signal was: Montgomery assumes command of Eighth Army at 1400 hrs today", whereas Auchinleck was officially to hand over command in two days' time, but in Monty's own words he seized command". He admitted: "I was issuing orders to an Army which someone else reckoned he commanded". Two years earlier, Auchinleck had reprimanded Monty for doing much the same thing. Monty was also a publicity-loving general. While on a visit to the front, he accepted the offer of an Australian slouch hat which provided greater protection from the sun than his own peaked cap. He asked for an Australian badge and fixed it on his hat. "When he visited the Indian and New Zealand divisions he asked for their badges too. This way he was seeking the Rommel effect. Monty the showman had arrived; while once the talk had been all of Rommel, now it was Monty", says the author.

General George Smith Patton was nicknamed "old blood and guts" because of his enthusiasm for battle. He was not only arrogant, egoistical and bigoted, but also used foul language. In the General's own words: "When I want my men to remember something important, really make it stick, I give it to them double dirty. It may not sound nice to some bunch of little old ladies at an afternoon tea party but it helps my soldiers to remember. You cannot run an army without profanity, and it has to be eloquent profanity. An army without profanity could not fight its way out of a piss-soaked paper bag". About

Rommel, Patton said: "It would be like a combat between two knights in the old days. The two armies could watch. I would shoot at him. He would shoot at me. If I killed him, I would be the champ. America would win the war. If he killed me...well... but he would not". At a hospital near Nicosia, the general came across a Private Charles Kuhl and asked him why he was there and was told, "I guess I cannot take it, Sir". The general raised him to his feet by the collar of his shirt and pushed him out of the tent with a final kick in the rear". After the American defeat at Kasserine Pass in 1943, Alexander wrote to Brooke: "They simply do not know their job as soldiers and this is the case from the highest to the lowest, from general to the private soldiers". Montgomery's view was that "It was lack of proper training allied to no experience of war, and linked with too high a standard of living".

General Johannes Erwin Eugen Rommel had concluded after the Great War that tactical victory depended on the on-the-spot decisions and rapid forward movement of frontline commanders. Hitler had personally selected Rommel to command the Deutsches Afrika Korps. He had told Mussolini that Rommel was the boldest Panzer Waffen (tank corps) general that they had in the German Army. Rommel had landed at Tripoli only six days after the British had taken Benghazi. He immediately ordered an advance. On 3 April 1941, he retook Benghazi as the British fled. The following day Rommel moved forward again and captured the British base at Mechili. It was from the fleet of vehicles left behind by the enemy that he took the Perspex dust goggles that were to become his mark, fixed from that day forward to the peak of his cap. Taking his lesson on the enemy from their retreat to the coast in Normandy, he pressed on full speed to prevent a second Dunkirk wherein earlier the British troops had made mass escape by sea.

After this event, Rommel was again the talk of all Germany. With his dash across North Africa, he had recaptured all the territory the British had taken from Italians. It was at this time that General Wavell's troops had started referring to Rommel as the "Desert Fox". The fennec is a small fox with a habit of burrowing quickly in the sand to escape predators. Its speed and ability to fade quickly into the landscape was a characteristic of General Rommel. Though Germany celebrated his latest blitzkrieg, Rommel knew that this victory meant little without destroying the British forces at Tobruk. The Afrika Korps reached Tobruk on 11 April and Rommel ordered an attack. Rommel is credited with an uncanny feel for what the enemy intended; but here he went wrong as the British had no intention to evacuate by sea. In fact, Churchill had said Tobruk must be held to the death without thought of retreat. The command at Berlin signalled Rommel to hold the ground gained and take no further action. Even though Wavell had launched operation Battle Axe, he failed to achieve anything. Hitler was elated and promoted Rommel to General der Panzertruppen (General of Panzer Troops).

The death of Rommel, however, is a sad chapter in military history. In the words of his wife Lucia Mollin: "My husband came to see me in the bedroom. It is impossible for me to describe what I saw in his face. 'What is the matter?' I asked. 'In fifteen minutes, I will be dead', he said absentmindedly. 'The Fuhrer has given me the choice of taking poison or going on trial before the People's Court'. He was suspected of taking a leading part in the scheme to kill the Fuhrer. He chose to take poison, because he was sure he would not reach the People's Court alive".

All in all, Terry Brighton's work is a commendable exercise for the lay reader. It combines the seriousness of war, the scholarship of history, the romance of biography and the flavour of literature. Had he been a military expert, instead of being a museum curator, he might not have produced such an interesting book!

Behind the Depression

WE ARE LIVING in a period which reminds us of The Great Depression eight decades ago. The British historian Arnold Toynbee had written, "In 1931, men and women all over the world were seriously contemplating and frankly discussing the possibility that the Western system of society might break down and cease to work". The economist John Maynard Keynes had said, "We are today in the middle of a great catastrophe—the greatest catastrophe due almost entirely to economic causes of the modern world". It was said in Moscow that this was the culminating crisis of capitalism and that our existing order of society would not survive.

The unprecedented economic progress of the 19th century and the early years of the 20th was founded on the gold standard. It was the anchor of most currencies; it provided the bedrock for banks and in times of war or panic, it served as a store of safety. The system was revered by banks in London, New York, Paris and Berlin. As a result, the commercial and financial linkages between countries were so extended that no country could rationally think of going to war.

In his book *Lords of Finance: The Bankers Who Broke the World* (2009), Liaquat Ahamed traces the efforts of the chiefs of the Bank of England, the Federal Reserve System, the Reichbank and the Banque de France to reconstruct the system of international finance after World War I. After a brief period when the world's currencies stabilised, cracks began to appear and the gold standard proved to be too rigid. Ahamed writes that four men in particular dominate this story; at the Bank of England was the neurotic and enigmatic Montagu Norman; at the Banque de France the xenophobic and suspicious Emile Moreau; at the Reichbank the rigid, arrogant but brilliant and cunning Hjalmar Schacht; and at the Federal Reserve Bank of New York, Benjamin Strong, whose energy and drive masked a deeply wounded and overburdened man. The story of the descent from the roaring boom of the 1920s into the Great Depression (1929-1933) can be told in many different ways. Here, the author has chosen to tell it by "looking over the shoulders of the men in charge of the four principal central banks".

The root of the crisis goes back to World War I. By the end of July 1914 the situation had escalated towards a general European war. With conflagration looming over the horizon, foreign nationals and commercial banks started withdrawing gold from their accounts at the Bank of England. Its bullion reserves fell from $130 billion on 29 July to less than $50 billion by 1 August. The war took its toll on the finances of the nations that were involved. Germany spent some $47 billion on its war efforts. Of this, 10 percent came from additional fares and the rest through printing of additional currency.

Britain spent $43 billion. An amount of $27 billion was raised through long-term borrowing, both domestic and foreign. Additional taxes provided $9 billion and the remaining $71 million came from the Bank of England. France incurred $30 billion on its war efforts; its middle class subscribed $15 million towards government bonds. An amount of $10 billion was given as loan by the US and Britain, and another $1.5 billion was raised through additional taxes.

During the Great Depression, the real GDP of major economies fell by over 25 percent. A quarter of the adult male population was thrown out of work. Major sovereign debtors in developed countries defaulted on payment of debt.

To quote Ahamed: "Part of the reason for the extent of the world economic collapse of 1929 to 1933 was that it was not just one crisis but, as I describe, a sequence of crises, ricocheting from one side of the Atlantic to the other, each one feeding off the ones before. Starting with the contraction in the German economy that began in 1928, the great crash on Wall Street in 1929, the serial bank panic affected the United States from the end of 1930, and the unravelling of European finances in the summer of 1931".

Ahamed agrees with the widely accepted view that the primary causes of the Depression were two: one, the politicians who presided over the Paris Peace Conference and demanded the exorbitant quantum of reparation that Germany was made to pay; and two, the return to gold standard after the War.

Lord Walter Cunliffe was supposed to be the most important of the three-man British delegation to the Paris Peace Conference. A hardliner, he suggested an upper figure of $200 billion as reparation to be paid by Germany to France and Britain. France's attitude was equally tough. This demand must seem fantastic if we remember that the annual GDP of Germany before the War had been estimated at about $12 billion.

The economist John Maynard Keynes was completely ignored by the British delegation. He wrote to Prime Minister Lloyd George that the battle was lost. Given the absurdity of these high demands being made on Germany, Keynes, then a young Cambridge don, came out in November 1919 with his thought-provoking book, *The Economic Consequences of the Peace*.

The book argued that in order for Germany to earn the money to pay Britain and France, it would have to sell more goods than it bought, and its main partners would have to be willing to absorb this large influx of goods with potentially crippling consequences for their own industries. It was therefore in the Allies' own self-interest to moderate their demand. In Keynes' words, "If Germany is to be milked, she must not first of all be ruined". Considering the capacity of Germany to pay and the ability of the Allies to absorb imports from Germany, Keynes suggested a reparation amount of $6 billion only. After a German default, the reduced sum of $12.5 billion was agreed to by the Allies, but even this amount was too high. In 1914, the German mark had stood at 4.2 to a dollar. By 1920, its worth was only 1.4 cents.

The second reason was the return to the gold standard after the War. Norman Montagu, the Governor of the Bank of England, thought that the gold standard was one of the pillars of a free society, like property rights or *habeas corpus*. Without the gold discipline, central banks would come under pressure to help finance their governments. A link with gold, according to Norman, was the only sure defence against a slide in the value of money.

What Norman and Benjamin Strong of the Federal Reserve had not realised was that there was a tectonic shift in the distribution of gold. The biggest hurdle to the return of the gold standard was the mountain of paper currency issued by the nations during the War. In England in 1913, the total amount of money in circulation was equivalent of $5 billion. This was backed by $800 million worth of gold. By 1920, money supply had ballooned to an equivalent of $12 billion whereas the gold reserves remained about the same. Thus, whereas in 1913 there was 15 cents worth of gold for every dollar in money, in 1920 each dollar was backed by less than 7 cents.

The alternatives to gold standard were deflation or devaluation. Britain took the route of deflation and Germany and France that of devaluation. The author points out that the biggest concern among the central banks after the war was not so much that gold was in short supply but that there was a major shift in its distribution. Before the War, there was a degree of parity between the stock of gold and the size of an economy. For example, the US, with a GDP of $40 billion, accounted for half the output of the four great powers—US, Germany, France and Britain—and held about $2 billion in gold, a little less than half of the total gold of these four countries. By 1923, the US had accumulated gold worth $4.5 billion. After the War, the three big European economies were left with less than $1.5 billion worth of gold in contrast to $3 billion before the War.

Keynes was of the view that the original rationale for a gold standard was the assurance that paper money could be converted into something tangible. That might have been necessary to instill confidence in paper currency at some point in history, but was no longer necessary as central banks were now capable of managing their countries' monetary affairs.

Author Liaquat Ahamed concludes with the remark that leadership was required to deal with the situation arising out of the aftermath of the War. After 1929, the responsibility for managing world money ended up in the hands of persons who lacked that quality. Strong had died in 1928; his successor did not have the personality or the stature to fit into his shoes. Norman and Sachet understood that a financial system in a free fall requires active central bank intervention, but both Britain and Germany were chronically short of gold. France had gold but Moreau was more interested in using France's new-found strength for political progress rather than for economic ends.

Lords of Finance is a lucidly written book. Its subject is serious and it has been made easy reading by using the style of an expert historian. The author tells the story and offers analysis without sounding harsh, or critical. An economist would like the book as would a layman. Liaquat Ahamed's presentation deserves to be read by anyone who wishes to understand the phenomenon of a market slump, whether caused by the irresponsibility of bankers or the myopia of politicians, or both.

What implicitly also comes through is that there are two capitalisms— that of production and that of finances or credit. Farms and factories earn by producing goods while the banks earn through lending money at maximum rates of interests. Often, they run on parallel lanes but sometimes do not. Ideally, of course, money should only serve as a lubricant to trade and industry. But the ideal is seldom practised, and the result can be an economic 'indigestion'—an uncalled for boom followed by a disastrous slump. If production were left alone, it would remain steady with marginal adjustments called for by changes in demand. There would be no convulsions, whether of 1929 or of 2008, or any other.

Looking back at Indo-Russian Trade

The Indian tea trade and industry is obsessed with the erstwhile Soviet Union, now called CIS market. For nearly 30 years, Indian producers enjoyed the "incidental generosity" of the Soviets. "Generosity", because the former Soviet government paid handsome prices, around 30 to 40 percent higher than the prevailing international level. "Incidental", because the rouble was falsely valued by the Reserve Bank of India. To illustrate, in 1997 the RBI treated the rouble as worth Rs 42, whereas it was not worth even 42 paise. The dollar was being publicly auctioned in Moscow at the time for some 3,000 roubles.

With the collapse of the Soviet Union and the end of the rupee barter trade, Indian tea exports have declined by up to one-third. The result is a slump in prices. Even now, so many years after the collapse, the tea traders live in the hope of a revival. It should, therefore, be interesting to pursue this nostalgia further back and recount the highlights of the Indo-Russian trade.

1897 was a year of interruption and anxiety in Indian tea exports to Russia. Plague had broken out in parts of the country and import of Indian tea into Batumi was, therefore, prohibited. Initially, the government reaction in Calcutta was one of anger and there was some talk of reprisals like stopping the import of kerosene oil pumped in Baku. The Indian Tea Association made a timely intervention and proposed that Russian authorities should be persuaded to recognise that tea is no carrier of plague. The crisis was fortunately short-lived. In the year 1903-04, nearly 29,000 pounds of Indian tea was exported from Bombay to Russia. Two years later, the quantity had trebled.

About this time, Percival Hodgson, the Chairman of UPASI (the United Planters Association of South India) wrote to the Indian Tea Association (ITA) that he understood from the British Consul at Selstan that there was a strong bias in Russia in favour of land-borne teas and such teas realised higher prices than their sea-borne counterparts. The ITA forwarded a copy of the Hodgson letter to E G Foley, its agent travelling on the Persian frontier. It also decided to send a copy to Colonel Yate, the Agent of the Governor-General in Baluchistan. The ITA also wrote to the London Committee to enquire as to the quality most favoured and the style of packing appropriate for the over-land route.

The Indo-Russian sea-borne trade continued to grow. A British Consular report of 1912 from the seaport of Odessa said that "the taste of the Russians had undergone an extraordinary change in the last decade". Their preference was swinging from Chinese to Indian and Ceylonese tea. Purchases from China had declined from 60 to 40 percent of the total imports. Due to rise in prices, imports via London were also diminishing and direct shipments from the subcontinent were more attractive.

The consular report went on to add that there had been an extraordinary increase also in the demand of green tea. Between 1904 and 1912, imports had grown nearly 20 times. Turkestan and the other Central Asian provinces had taken to green tea as a kind of substitute for intoxicants, which were forbidden by Islam. A whole new market, over and above that of black tea consumed by the European Russians, had been created.

When everything was hunky-dory, World War I ended and there was a general recession. But the crash in tea prices was unprecedented. Between the Christmas of 1919 and of 1920 the quotation for common teas had dropped in London drastically. In course of a year, the prices had become one-third. This slump was attributed to the Revolution and the Civil War in Russia. Imports by this great consumer had stopped all of a sudden. Much more tea had been shipped to Britain. Warehouses not only in London but also in the provincial towns were choked, as a lot of the common variety became unsaleable.

In due course, the Soviet Union resumed imports on a limited scale. An alternate home had not, however, been found for the surplus tea even a decade after the end of the Russian civil war. The annual imports by this country around 1930 ranged between 50 and 55 million pounds when contrasted with the pre-WWI figure of 200 million pounds. Trade circles in London felt that to save the industry from ruin, an urgent outlet for 50 to 100 million pounds had to be found. Writing in *The Capital* of 2 July 1931, the journal's London correspondent recommended that the USSR was the obvious home for this surplus quantity. This country was willing to import more, provided it was granted long-term credit. Russia had a good record of meeting its obligations and, therefore, there should be no hesitation in granting it credit terms. Apart from relieving the glut, what worried the correspondent was the danger of a whole generation growing up in Russia without being able to acquire the tea drinking habit. The supply of tea was dismally inadequate to go round at a price that would make it possible for most people to purchase it.

The Ceylon Association was reported in October 1931 to have turned down the proposal from the Ceylon Estates proprietary Association to extend two years' credit to Russia. The reason ascribed for this refusal was that a single Soviet agency bought all the tea. In the event of a default, the loss would be total and, therefore, unbearable. Statistics continued to be presented to the government to show how serious a factor the loss of the Russian market was. A July 1932 report from London complained that the Russian import of Indian tea had dropped from 55.5 million pounds in 1913 to only 11 million pounds in 1931.

The International Restriction Scheme and the consequent control over production helped to achieve a balance between supply and demand; prices improved and the market returned to normal. Yet Russia continued to preoccupy the attention of the industry. The zealots of the Empire were against any Dutch or Indonesian tea, in excess of the Restriction Scheme, going to Russia under a bilateral arrangement. The more broad-minded, far-seeing elements in London, however, took a different view. They were anxious about the disposal of the extra 250 to 400 million pounds that would come on the world market after the Restriction Scheme ended.

On 14 June 1934, the London correspondent of *The Capital* wrote: How any producer can stand out against the sales of black tea to Russia, irrespective of from which country it comes is beyond comprehension when for the last three and a half years we know the approximate quantity of tea that will be available from the chief producing countries. And consequently, if more Dutch tea goes to Russia there will be less to go to the other parts of the world and Ceylon and Indian tea will take its place.

In the meanwhile, negotiations between the producers and the Soviet government had been going on. The purpose was to ensure continuity of sales of black tea to Russia. The supply was plentiful and the Soviets were keen to buy more and more. The missing link was money and, therefore, credit had to be organised. It was at last in July 1934 that a tentative agreement and a scheme of credit were formed. A joint trading company was to be formed by the producers of India, Ceylon and the Dutch Indies. The owners of about 59 percent of the production of these countries were to subscribe to the share capital of the company on the basis of £3,750 million of tea grown. £938 were payable in cash and £2,812 were to cover any default by the Soviet government. As *The Capital* of 26 July 1934 reported: 'This would have provided a cash capital of £468,750 and with the uncalled balance of £1,045,000, would be sufficient to finance sales up to 30 million pounds per annum; and as the tea would be mostly bought on the London market would benefit every estate equally owing to the strengthening of prices as a result of such purchases'.

The joint company was probably to be known as Anglo-Russian Tea Trading Company, which would buy tea for cash at the auctions in London, Colombo, Calcutta and Amsterdam and sell it in Russia on 12 months' credit. The growers of India, Ceylon and the Dutch Indies were free to subscribe to the capital directly or through the respective holding companies. The governments of these countries would be asked to guarantee credits and, if necessary, to levy acess. The talks had proceeded so far that they raised high hopes but these were dashed to the ground when the negotiations were suddenly suspended. The resulting pessimism was widespread, although soon after, Russia returned to Mincing Lane as a buyer even if on a small scale. Arrangements were made for samples to be sent to Moscow in time for orders to reach London for the auctions each week.

As if to make the best of a bad job, JH Bunting, at the 1933 annual general meeting of the Indian Tea Association in London mooted the idea of propagating Indian, Ceylon and Java (Dutch) teas in the Soviet Union. This step could possibly counter the increasing exports of Chinese and Japanese teas to that country. The difficulty, however, lay in the fact that retailing in the Soviet Union was a government monopoly. Promoting particular growths that might not be made available to the consumer could prove not only wasteful but also counter-productive.

Addressing the Indian section of the Royal Society of Arts in 1936, EA Watson, Chairman of the Indian Tea Association and the moving spirit behind the earlier negotiations with the Soviet government, expressed the hope that the time would not be far distant when the Russians could again take a quantity similar to what they used to pre-WWI. He was so optimistic because 'they were naturally a tea drinking people'. Not all the listeners agreed with Watson and they felt that he had overlooked the fact that since the Russian Revolution a whole generation of Russians had grown up who knew nothing about tea and had never tasted the delights of the samovar.

Others, however, shared Watson's hopes and appreciated his untiring efforts to send more tea to the Soviet Union. In a 1943 issue of the *Tea and Rubber Mail*, it was stated that the future held more promise, and Watson's exertions on behalf of tea would not have proved fruitless if peace was won. It said, 'The Russian market alone would have proved the salvation of the tea industry'.

In June 1944, it was reported that the Soviet Union had received more than 35 million pounds of Indian and Ceylon tea through the British Ministry of Food. The trade, therefore, wondered whether the Russian market might be reopened. *The Manchester Guardian* expressed the opinion that there was a bigger opportunity after the war for developing the Russian market, given patience and a suitable approach, than expanding the American market, where the tea trade conducted a large advertising campaign in competition with coffee.

On 12 July 1948 at New Delhi, the first Indo-Russian food agreement was signed. India would receive 50,000 tons of wheat. In return it would supply 11.5 million pounds or 5,000 metric tonnes of high grade tea. The Tea Controller for India, acting for the government, soon invited offers for the supply of 4,250 tons of North Indian tea from the 1948 crop. Of this quantity, 60 percent was to be Assam, 30 percent Dooars, 5 percent each Cachar and Darjeeling, divided into 30 percent whole leaf and 70 percent broken. The prices and the procedure were to be similar to those that applied for supplies to the British Food Ministry.

In order to offset the quantity under the wheat-for-tea barter agreement with the Soviet Union, the Government of India, in 1949, contemplated a reduction in the shipments to Britain. The Soviet purchases removed from the Calcutta market tea of a quality suitable for Canada and the USA. Some in the trade felt that this would put Indian tea at a disadvantage in the hard currency markets. This conflict between barter and hard currency trade increased as the volume of trade with the Soviet Union went up. In the agreement signed in 1949, 200,000 tonnes of wheat and 100,000 tonnes of foodgrains were to be exchanged for tea, jute and castor oil.

A Losing Crusade

Christopher Caldwell is an American journalist who writes in leading newspapers like the *Financial Times*. In the course of 12 chapters stretching across 365 pages in his book *Reflections on the Revolution in Europe*, he portrays the anxiety and the agony which afflicts native Europeans today. The anxiety is that Europe could well cease to be culturally as well as racially what it has been. The agony is due to their helplessness in responding to the revolution set off by fast multiplying immigrants from Africa and Asia. As the author mentions on page 186, the native Germans have a fertility rate of 1.36 children per woman, whereas the Turkish immigrants appear to multiply at the rate of 2.4 children per woman. Eighty percent of young Turks are married whereas in the state of Westphalia only 32 percent of German natives tie the knot. Caldwell sums up the situation in the words, "The closer one gets to European culture, the farther one goes from family and its raison d'étre, children".

Eminent historian Arnold Toynbee attributes the practice of restricting the size of family, by abortion or infanticide, as a principal cause of the social and political downfall of the Greek civilization. The growth of this civilization was terminated by the trauma of the Peloponnesian War (431- 404 BC) fought between Athens and Sparta, which eventually engulfed nearly every Greek city state. It was a fratricidal war which in due course led to the disintegration of the Hellenic world. Modern Europe witnessed two enormous wars, the world wars, in the 20th century. Could they have induced the current decline of Europe?

An outstanding feature of the continent in its centuries of growth was nationalism and a competition between nation states. The horrors of World War II discredited nationalism as leading to racialism, militarism, chauvinism or patriotism. The institution of marriage appears to have suffered a collapse and has been replaced by live-in couples who produce very few children. Not only has homosexuality spread, even marriages between gays and lesbians have been legitimatised. To add to these woes came the challenge of migrants. Professor Toynbee has also stated that a society does not ever die from natural causes but always dies from suicide or murder; nearly always from the former. Unless circumstances change, Europe appears to be proceeding in the direction of both.

To make sure that the immigrants' identity is not diluted and the tradition of large families is maintained, a majority of immigrant young men marry women born in their home country. For example, over 60 percent of Pakistanis and Bangladeshis marry girls born in Pakistan and Bangladesh. Such marriages are evidence of a choice against assimilation into the European mainstream. Distinguished demographers,

David Coleman and Sergei Scherbakov, have been quoted in the book: 'Marriage migration in Britain has increased pro rata with the growth of the young age-groups of the Asian ethnic minority populations. That a preference for marrying foreigners should not increase is a dismal surprise. It might not have been so had these scholars realised that Islam's ultimate weapon lies in the women's prolific womb'.

The contention of the immigrant young men generally is that girls who grow up in Europe become distant from their own culture or become degenerate. The general impression in Denmark is that the immigrants migrate just because they want a better life; they do not necessarily want a European life. They want a Third World life with a European standard of living. The controversy over the head scarf to the tighter *hijab* (black dress) to the *naqab* (face veil) revealing only the eyes, to the big black *abaya* to ultimately the *burqa*, is well-known.

Native Europeans view the veil as a banner of solidarity with a violent international political movement that believes in and resorts to terrorism. But those who are Islamists or identify with them consider such garments as protection of the modesty, chastity and even the virginity of their womenfolk. When Ayaan Hirsi Ali, an immigrant from Ethiopia and now a Dutch citizen, made a case for the liberty of women from Amsterdam, the retort was that her city is known as a place where young women are allowed to sit naked in windows waiting for men to pay them for sex. Islamists are also aware that Christians, the Roman Catholics particularly, were equally emphatic about chastity as well as pre-marital virginity. They, therefore, feel that the native European reaction to Islam is motivated by wanting liberation from religion per se; it does not matter whether it is Christianity or Islam.

Another aspect of this problem is that immigrant boys are generally not serious about studies and often end up doing jobs like those of a taxi driver. On the other hand, the Europe-born migrant girls are serious and a number of them get well-paid white-collar jobs. Hence, too, there is a reluctance of boys to marry locally brought up girls. Be that as it may, it only accelerates the demographic revolution whereby the number of immigrants rises against the background of the native European population falling.

Going back into history, Christianity provided the basis of a political ideology until the Reformation which began in the 16th century. There grew up a number of churches and Christianity began to be divided. The excesses of the Roman Catholic priesthood were exposed and the political classes started throwing off the yoke of the Church on the State. The two were separated to give birth to secularism, which in turn, obtained ideological support from the Enlightenment. This celebration of reason led to the blossoming of modern European civilization whose outstanding heroes ranged from Sir Isaac Newton to Copernicus to Rene Descartes, Jean-Jaques Rousseau, Voltaire, John Locke et al. As reason flourished, faith diminished and the proportion of worshipping Christians declined.

Europeans became more intellectual and less Christian. Even the faithful appeared to lose some of their collective pride in their religion. The author quotes Islamologist Hans Jansen as talking of the end of religion. Amongst natives, religion shows signs of being a thing of the past. A poll by the influential paper *Le Figaro* found that 45 percent of self-described Catholics in France were unable to answer what Easter celebrates. In 2003, a Lutheran Pastor of Copenhagen had to be suspended for declaring that he didn't believe in God the Creator! In contrast, Islam is brimming with vigour and faith in Allah being the only God, there being none other. Most Muslims are Muslims first, Muslims second, and everything else later.

Pope Benedict XVI gave Islam a grudging compliment in the words: Islam's strength comes mainly from people's conviction that Islam can provide a valid spiritual foundation to their lives. This was the Pope who provoked an uproar of Muslim protest by stating that in Islam God is absolutely transcendent, not bound even to rationality. Little wonder that in France it was found that 85 percent Muslim students stressed that their religious beliefs were very important. Only 35 percent non-Muslims felt so ardently. In Germany, 81 percent Turks were religious against only 2 percent native Christians.

The European dice is thus loaded against the natives. Although Islam is today described as Europe's second religion, it is likely in the foreseeable future to become the first! Hence, Christopher Caldwell asks, "Can Europe be the same with different people in it?" This is the crux of the demographic revolution taking place with fully-aware native Europeans watching it helplessly.

This is not the first time that native Europeans are confronting Muslims. The first face-off began in 711 AD, when the Muslim Moors invaded Spain. Thereafter, the sword of Islam hung over Europe for a whole millennium until the second siege of Vienna by the Turks was defeated. The Christian will must have inspired the defence. That will appears to be weak today.

Every society or civilization changes with time and

circumstances. Perhaps, most native Europeans would be reconciled to the changing demographic profile of their continent, provided most or all of the immigrants were congenial to the ethos of Europe. Unfortunately, Islamists have been found to be determined to stick to their orthodox ways. In fairness to them, it must be said that Muslims are unchanging even when by themselves whether in Arabia, Iran, Pakistan, Bangladesh or India. They are reminded regularly by their imams that Allah is the only God and that Prophet Muhammad was the last prophet who delivered the final message of Allah. The implication is that a final message cannot be altered. Between the Quran, Hadith and the Sunnah, every answer is given for what to do, when to do et al.

What native Europeans find the most abhorrent about Muslims is their attitude towards women. They are not looked upon as equal human beings. Their two main functions are the pleasure and service of man or husband, and secondly, to produce as many children as possible. Then of course, there are practices of different ethnic groups which are found to be disgusting by even non-Europeans. For example, female circumcision (stitching the vagina shut) is practised by those who hail from Somalia, Sudan and to a lesser extent, Egypt. Moreover, the high premium on virginity has led to a number of controversies. To quote from the book under review:

> In the Netherlands, repair of broken hymens was often
> covered by national insurance until the ministry of health
> abolished it in May 2004. A scandal erupted in Britain in
> 2007 upon the discovery that the National Health Service
> had paid for dozens of 'hymen replacement operations' over
> the previous two years. Britain's *Daily Mail* interviewed

one doctor who specialised in such operations, including pre-wedding ones in which 'a membrane is constructed sometimes including a capsule of an artificial blood-like substance'. Honour killings appear barbaric to the natives of Europe, but they are practised routinely, especially by the Kurdish and Pakistani communities. Brothers murder their sisters or fathers kill their daughters for some trespass against sexual propriety—usually either wearing Western clothing or dating Western men. There were forty-five such murders in Germany alone in the first half of the decade according to a 2005 study by the Federal Criminal Investigation Agency. In Berlin, Hatun Surucu 'dishonoured' her family by dating a German and raising a child on her own. Her spectacular killing by several of her brothers in broad daylight in early 2005 was one of a half-dozen honour killings that year in Berlin alone.

One chapter is titled "Fear Masquerading as Tolerance". The implied thrust of the message is that the native European response to the immigrants is a mixture of their liberalism and their fear of Islam. It is difficult to tell which is greater. But neither is an effective answer to the immigrant challenge. Incidentally, the problem is substantially confined to Muslims. There is no mention of Christians, Hindus, Buddhists and others who have also migrated to Europe. Evidently these communities are comparatively docile and certainly not politically turbulent.

The Enlightenment as well as the recent horror of war led to an intolerance of intolerance—a mindset that has been praised as anti-racism and anti-fascism, and described as political correctness. Another factor that complicated the situation was the dread of communism right through the 20th century. One answer to the Red menace was a declared commitment to individualism, democracy, freedom and human rights, all of which justify a liberal attitude.

An interesting illustration of the fear prevailing in post-war Europe was given by Enoch Powell in his well-known 1968 speech called "Rivers of Blood" on the subject of immigration. He received hundreds upon hundreds of letters appreciating what he had said. But most of them omitted their address presumably because it was dangerous to do so; they could risk either penalties or reprisals if it were found out that they had praised Powell's opinion. As the author puts it, more and more native Europeans are becoming politically correct when they talk about immigration and ethnicity. The question is: Has the European public assented or submitted, been convinced or coerced into acquiring manners or losing liberties?

All in all, this book on the demographic revolution in Europe by an American, Christopher Caldwell, is an objective, masterly exposition on the low but chronic horror that afflicts Europeans. The volume should be read not only by those interested in the future of Europe but also those concerned with what lies in store for India. Our country also faces the dilemma although does not feel its pain due to the immunity developed over eight centuries.

In Pursuit of Truth

Logicomix is an extraordinary experiment of a graphic novel with Lord Bertrand Russell, a most outstanding intellect of the 20th century as its hero. It is the work of four Greek persons of proven talent, two in mathematics and two of them artists in cartooning and animation. To portray such a tall intellectual in cartoons must have been difficult enough and more so to lucidly tell the story of his epic search for truth with the help of mathematics and logic.

Although the book comprises 347 pages, the moral of the story of Russell's search is told with the help of some 1,400 colour cartoons drawn across 332 pages. The entire volume has been printed in Italy on art paper to bring out the colours as well as to hold the interest of even the youthful reader. Russell generally wrote in simple layman's language; nevertheless, the subjects he tackled are the most complex. Yet, the Greek artists have succeeded in portraying the struggle in simple interesting cartoons, as simple as seen in children's comic books.

Anyone at all interested in trying to understand life, its reality and its meaning for human beings should read this extraordinary work on Bertrand Russell. The novel or the story, neither a biography nor a history, begins with a university lecture in the USA. World War II had just begun and the American audience was apprehensive of Russell pleading for US help and involvement in the war in Europe. They were surprised when he declared that war was a most irrational phenomenon. He had consistently been anti-war. He was one of the few Britons who had supported Chamberlain and Daladier, the Prime Ministers of Britain and France, in September 1939 when they let Adolf Hitler gobble up Sudetanland, the western district of Czechoslovakia. This proxry surrender was hailed by both premiers as "peace in our time" achieved at Munich. Within ten months, the world conflagration was unleashed with the invasion of Poland by Hitler and Josef Stalin. The year 1940 saw the defeat of France by German tanks and the Battle of Britain brought on by Nazi bombers. Yet Russell, the British mathematician-cum-logician-cum-philosopher stuck to his anti-war platform of assumed rationality.

To the dismay of Russell, ever since the advent of Hitler, violence had begun to escalate—whether against the Jews in Germany or the recapture of the Rhineland in the face of Anglo-French anger; or the takeover of Sudetanland first and then the rest of Czechoslovakia, later followed by the Anschluss or the merger of Austria into Germany. Then, as we have said above, began the actual war. In the course of the early years of the war, Russell was arrested and had to stay in prison. He had repeatedly made statements against the war, which to the British government sounded unpatriotic and anti-national.

It was with the progress of the war that Russell realised that the alternative to war would be the handover of Europe to the barbaric designs of Adolf Hitler and Josef Stalin. His mind continued to battle between the search for truth and the reality of war, which was not rational. In the end, the great logician had to admit that there was no royal road to truth. To quote Russell: "If even in Logic and Mathematics, the paragons of certainty, we cannot have perfect assurances of Reason, then even less can this be achieved in the messy business of human affairs, either private or public".

What a disappointment this was to Russell who had placed so much faith in truth and reason. An illustration of his search for truth was his famous Russell's paradox which pulled the carpet from under mathematician Gottlok Frege's landmark work called *Foundations of Arithmetic*. Frege's reaction after he remembered the paradox was to put an addendum to the book. It reads:

"Hardly anything more unfortunate can befall a scientific writer than to have one of the foundations of his edifice shaken after the work is finished. I was placed in this position by a letter of Mr Bertrand Russell just when the printing of this volume was nearing its completion.

"The collapse of one of my laws, to which Mr Russell's paradox leads, seems to undermine not only the foundations of my arithmetic but the only possible foundations of arithmetic as such". On seeing the addendum, Bertrand Russell commented "There cannot be greater intellectual courage than this: to put the truth above all else".

From the beginning, the great philosopher's life was a quest for the foundation of mathematics. By studying the subject, he had hoped to penetrate the essence of truth. Mathematics, to him, was the queen of sciences and Euclid had taught him to abhor contradiction. Geometry had showed him the way towards reality, and reason was the royal road to truth. To Russell, religion was a house on sand, and was sinking; he had become an atheist despite his grandmother's efforts to inculcate in him faith in God. In spite of his genius, the great man lost his way; for example, the World War proved inevitable despite being utterly irrational. Could it be that he might not have lost his way had he also studied Eastern, especially Hindu philosophy? He had written a very successful book titled *The History of Western Philosophy* but he appeared to have made no mention of Eastern philosophy, which has relied more on inductive logic, whereas the West has placed its reliance on deductive logic. The ultimate and absolute premise of the Semetic religions, Judaism, Christianity and Islam is that God created the world in six days and rested on the seventh. These religions flow from this great premise set out at the beginning of the Old Testament. In Russell's own words, used in some other context, "If the premise is weak, so is all the rest".

In the West, logic has been called the study of methodical thinking, deduction and demonstration. The father of logic, Aristotle's classic *Organon* has discussed the study of deductive patterns called syllogisms which were synonymous with logical thinking. In simple terms, deductive logic argues from the premise above to conclusions and corollaries below; it rejects any contradictions on its path. For example, if the logician has seen only red roses, he would not accept roses of other colours as roses. To him, the pink, white or yellow are either other flowers or weeds. To the Hindu, all the colours would be possible roses and, instead of rejecting the other colours, he would say that maybe the other person is right based on his experience. That is inductive logic which argues from data at the bottom to the conclusion above.

Had Bertrand Russell given some space to Hindu philosophy, his search for truth might have been more fruitful. Without data, the Hindu tradition does not assert. Contrast the Semetic assertion of the world's birth with the Hindu view of *anaadi anant* (there is no beginning and no end); or the Hindu concept of God, *tattvamasi* or the *atma* or the soul and parmatma or total soul (God) are the same.

INDIA AND POLITICS

A Yatra of Hindudom

There is a new interest in the print media in democracy. The credit for introducing universal adult franchise must go to Jawaharlal Nehru. It was a bold move; whether it should have been taken so soon after Independence, within five years, is a matter of opinion. Until 1946, the electorate was only 13 percent of the country's then population; over a period of time, the eligibility to vote came to be extended to all adults of 21 years or more. This jump should be seen in the light of the prevailing literacy levels and the lack of experience with voting of most of the electorate.

One observes that the BJP is also participating in the debate on democracy on behalf of its parent, the Bharatiya Jana Sangh, which was founded as late as 1951 when the first general election was to be held the following year. The Constitution was promulgated in 1950 and Nehru might not have had the boldness to venture going to the people so soon after Partition, especially with the killings that accompanied it. Hindus mostly detested the division of the country; Gandhi had declared that it could take place only over his dead body.

The Hindu leaders in the Congress, whether Nehru or Sardar Patel, feared that without a partition, the Muslim League would launch a civil war. Their members were *au fait* with the knife from childhood, habituated as they are to reading the *kalima* just after slightly cutting a sacrificial goat's throat and then waiting for its life to go out. Without this ritual, there would be no *halal* meat. Moreover, in the army, prior to Independence the Muslims dominated in numbers, although they were only one-fourth of the country's population. In any case, most Hindus are averse to shedding and seeing blood. The threat of Jinnah was clear—Partition or civil war. He was especially clear in the presence of Viceroy Mountbatten.

Gandhi did not protest against Partition even by going on a fast, leave alone implementing his threat of "Partition only over my dead body". As a reaction to hordes of refugees coming in from the eastern wing of Pakistan, Dr Syama Prasad Mukherjee accompanied by Dr Rajkumari Amrit Kaur went to meet Mahatma Gandhi on 29 January 1948. The former appealed for implementing the plan of exchange of population, which Jinnah had earlier proposed. The Mahatma's reply was that the country's division had taken place "on the basis of territory" and "not related to religion". So nothing could be done. In short, Gandhi was not prepared to listen; this gives an idea of his obstinacy. Unfortunately, the next day he was assassinated.

Politically, all that needed to be done by the Hindus was to have expressed their condolences by attending his funeral. It was not a national calamity to justify any drastic reaction.

If at all, the assassination conferred martyrdom on Gandhi, who had been sidelined even by Nehru, Sardar Patel and other Congressmen. As fate would have it, the then Hindu leadership panicked. Dr Mukherjee resigned from the Hindu Mahasabha. He began the search for an alternative party which turned out to be the formation of the Bharatiya Jana Sangh with the help of Guru Golwalkar, who agreed to lend two reliable workers from the RSS per province; they would be whole-time workers of the new party.

The Jana Sangh contested the general election of 1952 and ended up winning three Lok Sabha seats. Their only small achievement was attracting a little over three percent of the votes polled, which gave it the recognition of a national party with the election symbol of a lamp. That was all. Instead, if the Hindu leaders had merely condoled Gandhi's assassination and returned to work as usual the following week, the results of the country's first general election could not have been worse than three seats. The Hindu leaders' panicky actions showed as though they themselves believed they were responsible for the tragedy and were, therefore, eager to wash their hands of the imaginary sin. In other words, they pleaded guilty to Gandhi's slaying, which simply was not true.

The reaction of Hindus not aligned to the Congress was that these leaders had no confidence in themselves and were, therefore, not worth voting for. Regardless, how much worse could the results have been than three seats? My own feeling is that they would have been much better. The Hindu Mahasabha would have functioned normally. In the elections, it could have harvested the votes resulting from the hated Partition and the cruelty perpetrated on the Hindus in both partitioned wings.

The enormity of the Hindu reaction was washed away by the tears for Gandhi's killing, for which except for small parts of Maharashtra, no one blamed them. Some Maratha goons beat up some Brahmins in those parts and set fire to their houses.

But more significantly, the Hindu masses lost confidence in their leaders for decades to come. The 1996 general elections were about the first elections when some confidence was expressed by the voters in a Hindu party they perceived as their own. Two years later, the first coalition government led by Atal Bihari Vajpayee was formed at the centre. A clear 46 years were lost by the Hindus. Even then, the leadership was hesitant and fielded a secular Hindu leader as prime minister. It was only Narendra Modi who was perceived as a trustworthy Hindu leader. Some observers began to talk of a Hindu vote bank, which was always there, but was lost by the apologetic attitude of the early leaders. If one takes 2014 as the year of the actual rise of Hindudom, 62 years were lost. If one counts the years of British conquests and rule, it would be another 190 years. The Muslim rule from Agra and Delhi added another 750 years of loss, except for what Maharana Pratap did in Mewar, and what Shivaji and the Marathas did, plus the achievements of Maharaja Ranjit Singh.

Not all foreign rulers were inimical to Hindus. But a foreigner is an alien and is not the same as one's own leader. The Nehrus, except for the last ten years, were Indian in nationality, but their rule was anything but Hindu. In fact, Jawaharlal Nehru, independent India's first prime minister, claimed to be culturally a Muslim—even his wedding card was printed in Urdu. The claim of Muslims was settled by Partition; in fact, if one considers those who did not leave and are still in India, more land than was rightful might have gone to Pakistan. However, the thrust of this submission is not land; it is all about self-rule or alien control and the chances the Hindus missed.

Now let us see what opportunity the Babri edifice offered and what the Hindus did with it. The real architect of the Ayodhya incident was the late Ashok Singhal of the Vishwa Hindu Parishad. The BJP leaders who had led the *rath yatra* to Ayodhya to reclaim the holy Hindu place lost their nerve within days of 6 December 1992, and some on the same day. This is why a look at the psyche of some Hindu leaders is necessary.

Regardless of the leaders' psyche, the Hindu masses, especially in north India felt that divine justice had been done. I doubt if it was ever a mosque. It had not a single minaret from which a muezzin could call the followers for prayers. While it is true that many a mosque in rural Turkey has a single minaret, presumably for the sake of economy, nonetheless the presence of a minaret is mandatory. At Ayodhya, a huge mosque did not have any of the normal accoutrements—no *wuzoo* for ritual washing of feet and hands before praying. It is doubtful if it had the *mimbar* (pulpit-like platform) for the imam to stand upon while delivering the *khutba* (sermon) every Friday.

It was more likely to have been a *dargah* built by Mir Baqi, one Babar's generals. He might have assumed it for himself when Babar died early. In the initial years, Babar was busy consolidating his conquests and he died within four years of his arrival in India. Mir Baqi might have meant it as an edifice for Babar, but in those days, it could not have been ready before his master died. In short, the whole incident appears confused.

Was it a *masjid* or a *mazar*? Was it for Babar's memory or for Mir Baqi's immortalisation?

Be that as it may, the cataclysmic events of 6 December 1992 yet again proved that the then Hindu leadership was neither willing nor prepared to rise to the occasion. The demolition of the Babri edifice was viewed by most Hindus as just retribution for centuries of Islamic tyranny, iconoclasm and persecution. Yet the BJP took an entire fortnight to even register its official stand on the event and when it finally did, the party officially distanced itself from the fall of the Babri edifice. Not only that, the party went on to lose assembly elections in Uttar Pradesh, Madhya Pradesh and Himachal Pradesh where it had been in power prior to December 1992. The reason was the party's perceptible distancing itself from the Ayodhya event; party cadres and the machinery were forbidden by the senior leadership from using the Ayodhya event to any electoral advantage. Ironically, even though the BJP failed to come back to power in these states, its total vote share exceeded that of its opponents.

This supposedly secular meandering continued throughout the decade of the 90s, which were also an era of coalition governments and politics. Perhaps the BJP internalised the media and intelligentsia narrative that "the BJP can never hope to come to power on its own because of its hard-line Hindutva ideology", and "coalitions are here to stay", and kept growing its distance from Hindutva. After the Atal Bihari Vajpayee government lost power at the centre in the 2004 elections, the BJP convened a *chintan baithak* (brainstorming meet), the National Democratic Alliance (NDA) convention. George Fernandes and Digvijay Singh of the Janata Dal (U) via a telephonic call, threatened to walk out of the NDA if the BJP were to persist with Hindutva. As a consequence of this threat by two non-ideological alliance members—not even part members—who themselves had little political weight, the then BJP vice-president quietly jettisoned the word Hindutva and promoted the softer term 'governance', which means little to the party's cadres.

The ideological drift, which cost the BJP the 2009 general election as well, added another lost decade to Hindudom's calendar. In the period 2004-14, India and Hindus had to endure a very hostile regime, whose animosity to Hindus was barely disguised. That reality, plus the growing realisation that a third term out of power could lead to Hindutva being more actively targeted forced the BJP leadership to unambiguously endorse Narendra Modi as their leader.

The Central Vista

The Parliament House where I sat until April 2000 made one feel welcome and important. It inspired me to participate with speech after speech. Our best speakers were in the Vajpayee ministry and could not debate; they could only reply or wind up debates. It is the non-ministers who had to do the debating and the routine speaking, plus asking questions. I attended every session day and generally sat until the house was adjourned for the next day.

I loved my mother and she reciprocated as I was her only child. When she turned 78, I wished she would live another 70 years or more, but she had become old and had a broken femur; it was better for her to go. I let her go gracefully and did not shed a tear. Life is growth and progress and change is the inevitable law. Parliament in the year 2000 was already getting old. The plaster and paint applied during the non-session time made it look elegant as rouge, powder and make-up make a lady pretty. Nevertheless, ageing was inevitable.

There were many committees and standing committee meetings and if the convener was not a VIP, we were allotted dingy little rooms on an upper floor. I wondered why in the first place such small rooms had been made. Then I discovered that a junior officer had vacated his room for the sake of the meeting; there was no other space for us. We were then a total of 795 members. This was the number in the 1950s when the population of India was 40 crore plus. Today, India is believed to have at least three times as many people.

I enquired from late CM Sahib Singh Verma the number of people he earlier represented in the Lok Sabha. His answer was at least 30 lakhs. Now the large constituencies must be unmanageably huge. It is high time the number of members increased to a thousand. The seating is close although comfortable. Now, we are under the shadow of Covid and the new spacing has to be more liberal, which means the halls should be twice as large. Similarly, all the other facilities—the central hall, the canteens, the library, the ministerial chambers, the committee rooms et al should be spacious.

The present Parliament House was to train Indian representatives to be legislators. They were expected then to legislate or even debate subjects. For those limited intentions, everything at Parliament was spacious. But time has not stood still nor has the clock stopped. A century has passed by and it has taken its toll. Those visitors who have seen only the ground floor might question the need to build again, but those like me who have toured the upper storeys would know what is overdue and what is not.

Reading the newspapers and watching the TV channels, I have found for months that the widely given advice is to spend money to distribute to the last man in the queue of poverty. Beyond a point, how does one distribute money except by spending it on public works as President Roosevelt of USA had done 1932 onwards? When it comes to political opposition, the leaders say how can you waste money on the luxury of the Central Vista when the Covid treatment needs the greatest attention? What an extraordinary contradiction between the economic masters, including Nobel Laureates on the one hand, and the national opposition?

The leaders of every era should leave behind some architecture that represents the ethos of that era. That is making, not writing, history. Muslim rulers were conscious of this requirement; the Hindus did build enduring temples but little else. Unfortunately, the iconoclasts in north India did not allow many temples to survive. In a way, some history was thus lost and we should be aware of this lacuna.

Those who have been inside the offices of Shastri Bhawan and its companions—Udyog, Nirman, and Krishi Bhawans know what they are like. The first floor of Nirman Bhawan has been refurbished very well, the rest I don't know. They were probably constructed in a hurry or cheaply or carelessly, or all three. That was done decades ago but we should put them right now. Europe gave great importance to architecture as the sentinels of an era. Look at the number of lovely state buildings in Mumbai and the statues of Kolkata which are now hidden at the back of Victoria Memorial.

Not as a lesson in iconoclasm but as the historical importance of architecture, let us quote Sir Arnold Toynbee, the great philosopher of history. "In the course of the first Russian occupation of Warsaw, the Russians had built an Eastern

Orthodox Christian Cathedral in the city that had been the capital of the independent Roman Catholic country, Poland. The Russians had done this to give the Poles a continuous demonstration that the Russians were now the masters. After the re-establishment of Poland's independence in 1918, the Poles pulled this cathedral down. I do not blame the Polish government for having pulled down the Russian church".

Opposition, Federalism and Democracy

A repeated criticism of the Opposition is that since the current government came to power in 2014, there has been a dilution in federalism, which in a large country is believed to be an important facet of democracy. The question is: has there been a dilution of democracy? The issue of federalism can be discussed subsequently. Elections, both central and state have been held regularly and on schedule. Covid or no Covid, polls took place in Kerala, Puducherry, Tamil Nadu and West Bengal.

There might have been President's Rule in one of our smaller states for a few days. Other than that, one can assert that Article 356 has not been used by the Centre and President's Rule has not been imposed anywhere. This is in contrast to even Jawaharlal Nehru who had used Article 356 to dismiss the state government in Kerala when Indira Gandhi was Congress president. As prime minister she made a habit of imposing President's Rule, with West Bengal being a particular target under its United Front government. Deputy Prime Minister

Chaudhary Charan Singh outdid Indira Gandhi. As soon as the Janata Party government was formed in early 1977, he dismissed all state governments that had a Congress ministry.

The most federal step that has been taken since Independence has been the introduction of the Goods and Services Tax (GST). Simultaneous with the levying of the tax, on a retail bill of even a hundred rupees, the GST is shared in half by the States and Centre. This means that as the GST is collected, half of it automatically goes to the States. This tax comprises virtually the entire indirect taxation of the country. Earlier, the former Planning Commission used to make an allocation annually when the state chief minister came to meet the Deputy Chairman of the Commission with a bouquet of flowers. This allocation had no accountability, nor was the amount of grant determined by any just and equitable measure.

Take the case of Article 370. Does its abolition not place all states and union territories on an equal keel? The birth of this Article was illegitimate. It was approved by the Nehru cabinet only and directly slipped into the Constitution as a purely temporary measure. The Parliament never saw the light of this Article. Years ago, an Englishman visiting India had asked me whether this was a special favour by a Kashmiri Prime Minister to the Kashmiris. What could I say in reply? Whatever may be the extent of federalism prescribed by the Constitution, it must be followed blindly.

The other aspect of federalism in practice is the quality of the regional politicians. Let us go back to the first two decades after Independence. Assam had Gopinath Bardoloi; West Bengal had BC Roy and Atulya Ghosh, Srikrishna Sinha and Anugrah Narayan Singh in Bihar, Chandrabhan Gupta in Uttar Pradesh, Pt Ravishankar Shukla in Madhya Pradesh, C Rajagopalachari and later K Kamaraj in Tamil Nadu, S Nijalingappa in Karnataka and so on. Compared with these tall leaders, we do not have many today. To a great extent they operated by principles, whereas today, national issues, whether health, defence of the country or foreign affairs are subject to party politics.

The latest example is the Covid-19 pandemic and the acquisition of vaccines. Some regional leaders probably thought that purchasing vaccines was a treat which the Prime Minister was monopolising. In response, the PM had declared that any state that chooses to acquire vaccines can do so. In two weeks' time, they found it to be a difficult task and declared that it was the Centre's duty to arrange for the vaccines. Such senior figures as state chief ministers ought to realise the difference between political and social issues to make a success of true federalism, and certainly not contradict themselves within a fortnight.

Many do not realise the differences between a union of states, federalism and quasi-federalism, or a unitary state. Also not realised is that there is a difference between a number of independent states voluntarily coming together to form a federation, as was the case with the USA. In India, basically, the British handed over to us a number of provinces; plus, there were princely states that were asked to merge with either India or Pakistan. There was no other choice except this option. Given the variety of our population, in Dr BR Ambedkar's view, the polity was such that India had to be more centralised than say, the USA.

It is noteworthy that the concept of federalism was born

with the inauguration of the US Constitution in the year 1781. During the times when monarchy was the general rule, there was no question of federalism. In Europe, except for Russia, most countries were of a medium size or smaller, hence the question of federalism. And Russia was an empire autocratically ruled by the Czars. Even democracy was not by any means a rule; it was Great Britain which stood out as a shining example of democracy. Germany took to democracy after World War I and by 1934, it was back to a dictatorship under Adolf Hitler. France began flirting with democracy after Napoleon was finally defeated and imprisoned on the island of St Helena.

Musings on the Uniform Civil Code

I insist I have the right to marry up to four wives at a time. If I wish to marry more I can divorce one of the current spouses and take on a fifth. Concomitant with my insistence, the law states that if I happen to be caught stealing someone's property, my hand would be cut off as punishment. My response would be, "No, no, no; the Indian Penal Code given by Lord Macaulay will be sufficient".

The Constitution of 1950 is satisfactory and all other laws are acceptable except when it comes to marriage and divorce. Article 30 of our national document allows me to follow my religion. Heads I win, tails you lose, because I am a spoilt child of the country. That is why I do not live in the state of Goa, where only one civil law applies. It does not admit the privilege of a spoilt child.

Actually, all other laws of my country are rational and correct. My grandfather decided we should stay back in India and not migrate to Pakistan when Partition was declared. When I grew up, my grandfather explained to me why he chose Hindustan over Pakistan.

Here, with Jawaharlal Nehru and hopefully his daughter in power after him, we could expect special treatment as their favourite children. The reason is that the great man was culturally a Muslim, so much so that his wedding invitation card, issued from Prayagraj (then Allahabad) was printed in the Urdu language. Moreover, he needed our vote because staunch Hindus would not touch him; they would go for the Jana Sangh.

No doubt, Article 44 of the Constitution has wanted a Uniform Civil Code (UCC), which also protects the rights of women, but my grandfather had assured me that this article would remain in cold storage for as long as we liked. It would indeed have been so, but for Nehru's grandson Rajiv Gandhi's blunder in passing the Muslim Women's Act 1986. Shah Bano was being awarded Rs 500 per month by the Supreme Court of India as maintenance after divorce. The Act diluted the judgement of the Supreme Court. Its memory would have faded out before long, but our leaders like Syed Shahabuddin, who were bureaucrats and not really clued in to politics, stepped in. Subsequently, without ever having visited Ayodhya, leaders like him took a strident stand over the Babri *maqbara*. It could not have been a masjid; it had to be a *maqbara*.

Firstly, there were hardly four years left of Babar's life after he came to India. His sidekick Mir Baqi would have been a Shia cipher without him. He had, therefore, claimed it as an edifice in honour of Babar. If it were a masjid, where was its *wuzoo* (place for ceremonial washing) and its *mimbar* (the Muslim cleric's preaching pulpit)? What did Muslims do when Hindus began their *puja* on the place's *chabutara* (platform) and later inside? Our leaders awakened and agitated the Hindus, thus bringing first AB Vajpayee and eventually Narendra Modi—who is committed to Article 44 and the UCC—to power. In my grandfather's words, had there been no resistance, the Babri issue wouldn't have burst into flames the way it did.

Does anyone realise that our Sharia helps to keep control over or rather acts as deterrence upon our womenfolk? It is like a concealed Damocles' sword over our married women, and thus maintains peace and balance in our community. As our Prophet commanded—and we obey—our community has been an expanding torrent. Another advantage has been that we have remained united. Unlike us, look at what happened to the Jews who have shrunk; or the Christians, who in the West have lost interest in the god who gave up his life on the cross for them. The only faith that has continually added to the capital of population is ours. Now, with the bringing in of the UCC, capital accumulation in terms of more and more children would cease. There are many countries whose capital is depleting. Japan, for instance, does not produce enough children nor allows immigration. I have heard it may have dwindling population in the coming hundred years.

They say democracy cannot function without secularism and uniformity of law. Furthermore, this Constitution guarantees equality for all citizens. But think of it, our community has flourished without any democracy, although with uniform law(s)—for ourselves. Actually, it is democracy that made India free and also made it a Dar-al-Harb (land where Islam does not rule). Until the beginning of 1858,

Bahadur Shah Zafar was the Mughal emperor; he was dethroned and exiled. India was a Dar-al-Islam (land ruled by Islam) till then.

Yet, many extremists go to any length and even quote Jawaharlal Nehru on this subject. The Hindu Code Bill became a law in 1955. Answering a Lok Sabha member's question, Nehru told Parliament: "Well, I should like a civil code which applies to everybody, but wisdom hinders. If he (the member) or anybody else brings forward a civil code, it will have my extreme sympathies. But I confess that I do not think that at the present moment the time is ripe in India for me to try and push it through. I want to prepare the ground for it".

Why Population Control is Necessary

The state of Uttar Pradesh has a little over 7 percent of India's land area but 17 percent of the country's population. In other words, the people in Uttar Pradesh live cheek by jowl. The second largest state, Maharashtra, in comparison, has 9.3 percent of the country's land area and only 9.28 percent of its population. Unlike UP, no other state in the country has such an adverse man-land ratio.

Yogi Adityanath, Uttar Pradesh's Chief Minister has apparently realised the adversity of the situation and has taken action in the form of the new proposed law, which in a sense amounts to *hum do hamare do*. A family planning law was brought in by Indira Gandhi in the 1970s for the entire country. In principle, her proposal did not provoke any great protest; actually, none at all. Its implementation by her bureaucracy being somewhat ham-handed drew opposition, which was muted because the Emergency was in force. When campaigning for the 1977 general elections began, protests by the Hindus in UP, (where I spent a fortnight to observe the electioneering), broke out.

One Shyamlal Tiwari, who was kind enough to join my friend Raju and me in the course of a morning at Prayagraj (then Allahabad), happened to tell us that he was a 56-year-old widower with four children. Yet, the police dragged him to a *nasbandi* (sterilisation) centre and forced him to undergo a vasectomy. Later, Tiwari took us to a colony where mainly Muslims resided. That was quite an experience. The protests there were so vociferous that one had to see and hear them to believe it. There were quite a few ladies who said that never again would they vote for the Congress. The party did not even know that their Holy Prophet had ordained them to bring forth more children. The Congress regime's government servants chased their young sons to force them to undergo sterilisation. In order to protect them, the womenfolk would get up at three in the morning, cook what they could and send the boys away with their food into the fields and farms for the day, telling them not to come back till after dark. "Tell us sir," they said, "is this a *hukumat* (government) with any *tehzeeb* (decency) or *tamaddun* (culture)?" Despite all their precautions, many a boy was victimised.

To offer a quick glance at the world population, today the planet has approximately 7.7 billion people. At some point, we must halt this human multiplication. I remember our Prime Minister Modi saying that India can enjoy a population dividend. He is right, provided the young Indians of today are able to become truly educated and realise their potential. To educate and empower so many people is a Herculean task.

The way Uttar Pradesh is going, leave alone education, there will be no space to even stand before long. Already there are about ten thousand people per square kilometre, and yet on television, Opposition spokespersons have been asking whether CM Yogi Adityanath has a 'communal' motive of introducing this two-child law. In fact, we all need to get together and spread this initiative across the country.

On the one hand, many of us are crying aloud about a change but none of us feels anxious about a change in climate resulting in, from time to time, a failure of crops and, thereby, food shortages. It is essential to insure ourselves schematically against a drop in food production.

Uttar Pradesh is one of the lesser industrialised states in the country. Its chief minister feels that it is the government's duty to fill up the lacuna and thus create a bigger base for increasing employment and, at the same time, enlarge the economy by increasing the gross domestic product. This can be achieved either by controlling the population or finding the wherewithal for creating new industries, more tourism, service sector et al. All this would require more and more investment to vastly increase the skills required. It is possible, but it would be a long journey. Population control certainly is a much easier and quicker process. The other path just described would appear a pipedream to many.

What indeed is a reality is what climate change is doing to countries. With this stupendous increase in world population, we occupy, more or less, the same land area. We cultivate about the same area of land. Is it surprising that the climate is changing towards the unpredictable? The earth is getting warmer. Imagine parts of Canada are experiencing 50° Celsius temperature. As a result, the sea level would rise and drown the coastal areas of many a country. It has been predicted that our neighbour Bangladesh will lose approximately 17 percent of its coast in about thirty years.

UP and Yogi Dynamism

India's largest state Uttar Pradesh, and also its most politically vibrant, has moved in the field of development the fastest. Whether in the layout of highways, appointments to government services, providing employment to the people; increasing investments, improving law and order, encouraging tourism and pilgrimage, as well as expanding the small and medium enterprises sector, Uttar Pradesh is making waves.

Since independence, one had never heard that this state had moved in the area of development. It is surprising that New Delhi did not bother, ignoring the fact that UP is one-fifth of India. If, therefore, UP leaps in progress, the country races ahead in terms of development. Evidently, for the powers-that-be in India's *rajdhani*, UP was treated as a bank of 84 Lok Sabha seats (now 80) and a sure-shot ticket to parliamentary majority at the Centre, but nothing more.

UP today, in 2022, is a vastly changed place. From the backwaters of most economic indices, the state today has moved to becoming India's second-richest in terms of gross state domestic product (GSDP), which stands at $268 billion, behind only Maharashtra now. This, under CM Yogi Adityanath has been an achievement despite the ravages of the Covid-19 pandemic. In the ease of doing business, (a crucial global benchmark), UP, which languished at 16th position in the country in 2016, has moved up to the second rank among India's states.

Law and order, the most important prerequisite for any development activity to flower, was never strong in Uttar Pradesh before Adityanath took over. Any economic or capital investment in the state remained a dream. The scenario after Yogi's coming to office in March 2017 is a sharp contrast. Over the past four and a half years, 137 criminals have been liquidated in police action; while close to 3,000 criminals were injured. Nearly 37,000 accused have been booked under the Gangster Act and over 500 under the National Security Act. The Yogi administration has also hit criminals hard by targeting their finances. In the state government's drive against the mafia, their illicit property worth more than Rs1,500 crores has either been attached or demolished. Along with action against the mafia, the Yogi administration has also provided protection to witnesses.

A vastly improved law and order situation has begun to pay off in the realm of development. Here, too, figures speak for themselves. The state's development data reveals that over the years, UP has received investment proposals worth Rs 66,000 crores from both foreign and local investors. The administration has acted promptly on these proposals. More to the point, companies from Japan, Canada, Germany, Hong

Kong, the UK, USA, Taiwan and South Korea are lining up to invest in UP; one company has left from China to set up operations in Agra. It is also significant that the government is ensuring that the flow of investment is not confined to the state's bigger cities, but is also being channelled to smaller towns like Etah, Amroha, Mirzapur, etc.

Apart from the fresh proposals for investment, MOUs worth Rs 4.68 lakh crores have been signed at investors' summits, of which 371 proposals worth close to Rs 3 lakh crores are already functional, generating employment for up to 5 lakh people. Here, one must make mention of the work being done by this government on the defence-industrial manufacturing corridor, which has already drawn in up to 14 MOUs. The aim is to transform Uttar Pradesh into a hub of capital-intensive manufacturing, which the defence industry invariably entails.

Farmers have much to be happy about in Yogi Adityanath's rule. Development schemes and programmes for their long-term success also need the health of the rural economy to be robust. The Adityanath policy of transparent purchase of wheat and paddy, as also his continuous supervision of purchase centres has been successful. The example of paddy should suffice; the state government has purchased a record 60 lakh metric tonnes of the grain, against a slated target of 55 lakh metric tonnes. Payments made to the state's farmers have been touching new records as well. The government has stepped up its efforts to double the income of the state's farmers. Nearly Rs 33,000 crores have been transferred to the accounts of the nearly three crore farmers under the Pradhan Mantri Kisan Samman Nidhi Yojana, plus separate transfers under crop insurance schemes. The modernisation of 20 sugar mills in the state, along with the reopening of the Pipraich, Munderwa and Ramala sugar mills is a particularly significant milestone in the Yogi administration's agriculture policy.

Uttar Pradesh under Yogi Adityanath is clearly not one of the "BIMARU" states it was once derided as, but a state on a rapid march upwards. Being backward is bad enough, but if one-fifth of the country is sick, the rest of the body cannot in any way be healthy. Moreover, the Narasimha Rao-initiated 1991 reforms did not benefit UP. This makes UP's march under Adityanath all the more remarkable.

The Opposition

The Opposition needs the legislature much more than the government. Ministers can pass bills in a few minutes at a time, especially if the Opposition does not pay attention to legislation and remains distracted by agitation. Rushing into the well need not necessarily provoke adjournments. A few agitating members can, upon the Speaker's orders, be dragged away out of the House by the marshals. This used to be done in the earlier years of Independence. Recalcitrant members were physically carried out.

Some Opposition parties and members just do not appreciate the gift the parliamentary floor is. The opportunity it gives to MPs to express themselves and their policy views is phenomenal. One reason could be that Opposition leaders do not study enough and do not, therefore, have anything substantial to say. The 2019 general election was fought by the leading Opposition on the slogan *"chowkidar chor hai"*, implying that the government had pocketed money from payments made to France for the purchase of Rafale warplanes for the Indian Air Force.

However, the Supreme Court declared the deal as clean. The Opposition allegation was based on the habit of politicians lining their pockets whenever a sizeable deal materialised. After the 2019 election results, one survey agency said the party bandying the *chor* slogan lost quite a few votes for repeating this slur ad nauseam. The ruling party could have easily countered this with "*Gali gali mein shor hai Rajiv Gandhi chor hai*".

Opposition parties should have a think-tank for national policies, which can help its leaders to introduce bills based on the think-tank's findings. Parties on benches should have shadow ministers, starting with a shadow prime minister (leader of Opposition), a finance minister, defence minister and so on. Informed and intelligent debates would then be possible. Parties then would be equipped with knowledge and ready on policies instead of shouting only allegations and frequently walking out. Currently, the impression is that they pocket hefty emoluments but do little work.

Once, the late Union minister Anil Madhav Dave had lunch at my home. The BJP was in Opposition then and did walk out occasionally. Our mutual opinion was that there should be no or rare walkouts. Whenever the BJP had a grouse against the government, its members should wear black armbands. Other methods of protest could be wearing half-black attire or members sitting in the aisles.

Right from the beginning, there has been no tradition of parliamentary party offices doing ideological or academic work. The Communist parties did something, but one doesn't know if they did any fresh thinking or merely repeated what Marx and Lenin said or wrote. Else, why were these parties clueless after the Soviet Union disintegrated in 1991? Nowhere in the world have the Communists found any alternative.

In Britain, not only do the Conservative and Labour parties (perhaps also the Liberals) have shadow ministers but also constituencies allocated to their members, who are supposed to be in touch with their constituency and are expected to hold small meetings, so that the party knows what is going on in each constituency. The particular member works as though he would stand from the constituency in the next election. This may not be possible for a party like the Congress, as early allocation of a seat could result in fights between various aspirants. The Congress, therefore, does last-minute allocations to avoid trouble.

The quality of political candidates in the West is overall superior to those at the bottom of the rung in India. Education used to be a problem earlier. Also, there is hardly any on-the-work training on the Constitution or parliamentary articulation.

A quick study of every new MP would be useful. There would be some well-travelled, knowledgeable MPs who would know quite a bit about the country. But most aren't aware of every nook and corner of India. Yet, they are elected to debate and legislate for the country. A brief history of post-Independence India and a quick look at the armed forces during the five wars we have fought must be provided in the two weeks during the first gap between two House sessions. This will make MPs well equipped to debate national issues. Minus this, Members either remain silent or talk nonsense.

In my years in Parliament, I came across some MPs

who for two consecutive sessions (ten years) did not speak at all. They were from Gujarat, and knew their state but not enough about other places. Two members I knew had asked for starred questions; they were excited about their chance to speak and rehearsed for several evenings. Their problem was language. They could hold huge crowds in Gujarati. They knew adequate Hindi to converse but not enough to make speeches in Parliament. There must have been many such sad specimens from other states who kept silent, talked nonsense or simply shouted down members on the opposite side of the House. When they got bored, they played a role in the adjournment of the House. There are other members who do not have a language problem, but suffer from knowledge-cum-information deficiency. Then there are others who talk loosely before the media. The anti-government media—whether Indian, American or European—laps this up to malign India in front of the world.

Netaji Subhas
and the Mahatma

Did India win Independence because of the non-violent movement led by Mahatma Gandhi or was it the impact of Subhas Chandra Bose's Indian National Army that made the British panic and leave India?

Most Indian history textbooks about the freedom struggle are dominated by the role played by the non-violent movement of Mahatma Gandhi. But was India's freedom gained entirely by the non-violent struggle of Gandhi and was there no contribution of the use of force?

Here, one ought to quote from a conversation between former British Prime Minister Clement Attlee and the then Governor of West Bengal, Justice PB Chakraborthy. In 1956, Clement Attlee had come to India and stayed in Kolkata as a guest of the then governor. Attlee was the man who as leader of the Labour Party and British Prime Minister between 1945 and 1951, signed off on the decision to grant Independence to India.

PB Chakraborthy was at that time the Chief Justice of the Calcutta High Court and was also serving as the acting Governor of West Bengal. He wrote a letter to the publisher of RC Majumdar's book, *A History of Bengal*. In this letter, the Chief Justice wrote: "When I was acting Governor, Lord Attlee, who had given us independence by withdrawing British rule from India, spent two days in the Governor's palace at Calcutta during his tour of India. At that time I had a prolonged discussion with him regarding the real factors that had led the British to quit India."

Chakraborthy added, "My direct question to Attlee was that since Gandhi's Quit India movement had tapered off quite some time ago, and in 1947 no such new compelling situation had arisen that would necessitate a hasty British departure, why did they have to leave?"

"In his reply Attlee cited several reasons, the main among them being the erosion of loyalty to the British crown among the Indian army and Navy personnel as a result of the military activities of Netaji," Justice Chakraborthy said.

That is not all. Chakraborthy added, "Toward the end of our discussion I asked Attlee what the extent of Gandhi's influence upon the British decision to quit India was. Hearing this question, Attlee's lips became twisted in a sarcastic smile as he slowly chewed out the word, m-i-n-i-m-a-l!"

Attlee's is not the only authentic testimony to what really happened between 1942 and 1947. There is further documentary evidence. Deep down in the 4th basement level in a temperature and humidity-controlled hall of the British Library near Euston Station, London, are stored the 'India Office Records'. These records are pretty nearly everything that the British colonial rulers had with them in India and were transported back 'in toto' before 15 August 1947. Amongst these records is a document penned by the then Commander in Chief in India, Field Marshall Sir Claude Auchinleck. It is a memo to the then Viceroy, Field Marshall Wavell. The purport of this extraordinary memorandum is that "…..Gandhi is not a problem. We can deal with him and handle him. The Congress is also not a problem. We can easily deal with them. But now that India and Indians know about the INA as also about the mutinies in the Royal Indian Navy and the Royal Indian Air Force, the Indians know that we have lost the love of the Indian Armed Forces. It is time to leave India!" As British historian and author Alex von Tunzelmann writes in her excellent book *Indian Summer: the Secret History of the End of an Empire*, neither Gandhi nor Congress party agitations forced British hands. It was the possibility of a full-scale military revolt due to the influence of Subhas Bose (and the INA) which led to the British exit from India.

There is no doubt that Gandhi initiated the freedom movement. His various symbols, such as his own attire, *charkha* and *khadi* and his Ratnam fountain pen, which was the first *swadeshi* pen, were symbols for those who wished to join his movement for independence. Without this awakening, it is possible that independence would have been put back by several decades. However, to assert that it was Gandhi who successfully led us to independence is stretching things way too far.

Having finally left South Africa to settle in India in 1915, Gandhi's first intervention was an agitation against the Rowlatt Act, which was deeply humiliating for the people of Punjab and all of India. But Gandhi could not compel the British regime in any way to withdraw the Act. Instead, ironically, the people of Amritsar had to endure the terrible Jallianwala Bagh tragedy, brought about by Gen Dyer's merciless firing on an unarmed crowd.

In 1920, Gandhi launched the Non-Cooperation Movement, the English term for his *satyagraha*. But while it had gathered momentum, some miscreants set fire to a police station in Chauri Chaura in UP, burning alive 22 police personnel. Such violence was completely against Gandhi's principles, and he simply ended the Non-Cooperation Movement. In other words, the first major anti-British movement failed.

Come 1930, and Gandhi launched the Civil Disobedience Movement on a grand scale. This included the Dandi March in which some salt was produced without paying tax. Other than extracting a few pounds of duty-free salt in exchange for losing a few Indian lives in British repression, the movement was a failure. In order to save his face and that of the Congress, Gandhi met the Viceroy and signed the Gandhi-Irwin Pact, which amounted to little. The Viceroy, for his part, in due course invited the Congress to the Round Table Conference in London. Gandhi attended the 1931 session of the Conference as his party's sole representative. The 1930 and 1932 sessions went on without Congress participation.

Under the 1935 Government of India Act, elections were held in all the provinces and the Congress won a majority of them. However, their ministries did not last long and in 1939, they resigned in protest against the British decision to involve India in WWII, which had broken out that year. This left the resulting vacuum at the mercy of the Muslim League. This was Gandhi's strategic blunder, though glorified as the Quit India

Movement of 1942, launched from Gowalia Tank, a small maidan in Bombay. Most Congress leaders were incarcerated, while Jinnah and his honchos did what they could to gain a hold over the Muslim masses. They threw all scruples to the wind; they claimed that the Hindu population of Assam was only 38 percent and the province's adivasis were not Hindus but 'animists'. The objective was to carry the province into the Pakistan they hoped to gain by dividing the country.

To sum up, Gandhi led four movements in a span of 24 years and all of them came to naught. When he came out of prison in 1945, the political environment in the country had changed. Gandhi was now merely a Bapu, with Nehru and Sardar Patel at the helm of Congress affairs. Nevertheless, he continued to hold his evening prayer meetings at 5 pm every day. In the course of one of them, he was assassinated. Had he survived, he might have lost his greatness in his lifetime.

British author Michael Brecher has criticised the practitioner of *satyagraha*. To quote: Of all the participants only Gandhi had a clear and consistent object—to oust Bose (*Nehru: A Political Biography*). Historian Michael Edwards wrote in his *The Last Years of British India*, that Gandhi, whom so many in India and abroad believed to be only sweetness and light, had by the use of his overwhelming prestige and not a little intrigue, succeeded in disposing of the only real opposition to his leadership.

Bose's radical agenda did not suit Gandhi who opposed him for seeking re-election as president of the Congress in 1939.

Nevertheless, in the polls that followed, Gandhi's candidate, Dr Pattabhi Sitaramayya, was defeated. The Mahatma could not stomach his candidate's defeat. In his book, *The Springing Tiger*, historian Hugh Toye has written: Bose's popular mandate as President of the Congress in 1939 was denied by intrigue—intrigue not only against him but against the very democracy that had elected him.

There is no doubt that but for Gandhi the masses of India might not have become aware, for many more years, about the importance of Independence. His genius at mass contact was unprecedented. When he started his movement, there were comparatively few highways and long distance land travel was confined to railways. There was no radio until 1927. In any case, the influential media was in the hands of the British. Yet, with the help of *charkha* and *khadi*, Gandhi was able to communicate and convey to mostly illiterate villagers what freedom could bring for them. In a matter of a few years, he was able to electrify the atmosphere with the need for *swaraj*.

So far, so good. However, Gandhi's contribution in precipitating the departure of the British was very limited. The British evidently understood the barrister's ways, however unconventional they were. They knew how to deal with his agitation and keep him at bay without taking any harsh measures. In any case, Gandhi himself was not in any undue hurry. His concern for early independence was not as great as his anxiety to outwit Qaid-e-Azam Jinnah and prevent Partition. This is evident from the 75-day talks he held with Jinnah at Malabar Hill, Bombay, during September 1944. The talks between the two leaders have been recorded by their correspondents and have been published.

The "Quit India" call of August 1942 and the incarceration of leaders in its aftermath consisted of the last phase of the Congress agitation against the British. On the other hand, the impact of the Indian National Army or the Azad Hind Fauj, founded and led by Bose had a telling effect on the psyche of the British rulers; not because the INA had proved to be a substantial military threat but because it was a living proof that soldiers who had sworn loyalty to the Crown could go back on their vow. The secret of the British rule had been that only about 100,000 expatriates could control an empire of 40 crore people (then). The rest of the officials who ran the empire's administration and manned its armed forces were Indian. What Netaji's INA did was to shake the British confidence in the continuing loyalty of not only the defence forces but also the civilian machinery. The British fears were vindicated when men of the Indian Navy mutinied at Bombay in 1946.

Netaji Subhas's action thus hit the Achilles' heel of the foreign rulers. They took it as a clear message that it was time to pack their bags and go. Gandhi awakened the Indian masses to the value of being free and stirred their souls to demand independence, but it was Netaji Bose who precipitated the British departure. This achievement of the "springing tiger" has not enjoyed the highlight it deserves. Nehru feared that Bose might not have been killed in the reported air crash at Taipei on 17 August 1945. Perhaps the Bengal tiger might return to compete for his power and popularity. In the bargain, Nehru made it his party's as well as government's policy to obscure and also obliterate the legend of Netaji.

Independence not only meant a great deal to India, but also set-off a chain of decolonisation across Asia as well as Africa.

In the wake of their decision to quit India, the British rulers evidently carried the policy of withdrawal to most of their other colonial possessions. From Ceylon in the south to Ghana in the west, the trend of decolonisation soon spread to other European imperialists, namely the Dutch in Indonesia, the French in West Africa, Belgium in Congo and, in due course, Portugal gave up Angola and Mozambique. In all, 42 countries became independent after India became free in 1947.

The Congress' Troubles

The Congress, India's once all-powerful party and its ruling disposition almost by default, today looks a shadow of its former self. Its leadership must realise that being India's oldest political party it has a duty towards the country. In turn, it is supposedly one of the guardians of democracy. Acquiring power and governing properly ought to come next in its order of obligations. As things appear today, the Congress is devoted to neither of these. It merely demonstrates and expresses blind hatred of Prime Minister Modi, which has no place in democracy. An opponent is an adversary, no more. Abuses like *"chowkidar chor hai"* betray the speaker's character and pollute the political atmosphere to no one's gain.

The Congress has mostly functioned on the Führer principle or the leadership principle. From 1921, Mohandas Gandhi continued to dominate the party until 1946. Then it was the turn of Jawaharlal Nehru, especially after Sardar Patel's passing away. He was followed by his illustrious daughter

Indira Gandhi and in turn by her son Rajiv Gandhi, who knew or understood little of politics, but managed somehow for five years. But he left a dent in the party. The poor man and woman ceased to think the Congress was their party. Under Rajiv, it had become the outfit of the rich who wore Gucci shoes, Ray-Ban glasses and so on.

However, even till then, no one looked upon the Congress as an anti-Hindu set-up. After PV Narasimha Rao completed his term in 1996 as prime minister, the party began to wobble. It seemed as if it was not being held together. The consensus emerged that only a Nehru-Gandhi could do so. Thus, Sonia Gandhi was fished out from virtually nowhere to take over the presidentship of the Congress. To many an objective observer, it seemed that she would not be able to cope with the job; but she did for ten years, not by hit or miss but by mediocre partiality. The secret was Ahmed Patel, who had been loyal to Indira Gandhi right through the Emergency. He was a young MP from Bharuch in Gujarat. He sat at 12 Willingdon Crescent bungalow outside Indira's workroom on a stool the whole day except during the lunch hour, when he went home. Presuming me to be a fellow sympathiser, he explained to me at the Circuit House, Ahmedabad, his reason for such unflinching loyalty. While he was not by any means a rabid Muslim, he felt that the future of Muslims in India lay with the Congress. No other party was dependable and capable of keeping this community across India, more or less united. And the Nehru-Gandhis were the only family under whose umbrella Congressmen could remain together. Hindu domination would ruin this *Dar-ul-Aman* (realm of peace).

Till Ahmed Patel was Sonia Gandhi's guide, friend and

philosopher, she could play the role of the supreme leader of the Congress and later that of an elder statesman in India. Trouble began for this cozy arrangement when Patel caught Covid and subsequently left the world.

Ahmedbhai was an epitome of political selflessness and was above the usual political desires. He was utterly loyal to the Nehru-Gandhis, and did not place any importance on becoming a minister; nor was he particularly fond of money. Above all, he never threw his weight around. Evidently, these are rare qualities in the world of politics. Then, he was a non-Hindu and, therefore, could easily fit into the mould of Sonia Gandhi's preferences. She could, therefore, blindly trust him as she indeed did.

For a foreign lady to understand the currents and cross-currents of India's diverse politics was almost impossible, especially if we take into account the fact that she had no political background. Oscar Fernandes could have been a useful replacement in the absence of Patel, but even he has quit the world. As we have seen, as an amateur of foreign birth, Sonia's demands for a political adviser are very tall. Herein lies the tactical problem of the present confusion and troubles the party finds itself in. The Opposition is bereft of a political strategist. All in all, for the present, it is a one-sided game. At the ground strategic level, the ethos of India has transformed from the Nehruvian to Hindu. What to do in this situation? The entire Opposition is roundly confused.

Socialism on the one hand, and the Hindu way of life and its priorities on the other, do not jell. The former, in Marxist terms, can be described as "from each according to his ability, to each according to his needs", whereas the Hindu ethos revolves around karma. The sum of a person's karma, including in past lives, determines his opportunities and the course of his life, not the state or the government. Non-alignment should not necessarily mean Nehruvian propensity to run and retreat, as he did particularly against China in the 1950s. In Kashmir, too, Nehru was reluctant to fire. The results are for everyone to see.

The current government's burden is to clean and clear the mess Nehruviansm has left behind. Its incompetence in ruling has been evident in every member of its family. We have seen Nehru's performance as well Rajiv's. Indira Gandhi's performance is also well known with regard to the 93,000 Pakistani prisoners of war let off in 1972 without forcing Pakistan to yield anything in return. Doubts remain regarding the wisdom of relieving Pakistan of its unwanted backyard, which commanded the majority of its then undivided population. This is a story that has yet to be told adequately.

MPLADS

MPLADS, or Member of Parliament Local Development Scheme, which allots Rs 5 crore annually to every MP, was suspended for the years 2020-21 and 2021-22, and for good reason. But several MPs feel the scheme should be revived. There are 543 Lok Sabha and 250 Rajya Sabha MPs, a total of 793. Each was last entitled to Rs 5 crore for this purpose. If fully utilised by every member, the Government of India would spend Rs 19,825 crore over five years (the Rajya Sabha's term is six years but let us ignore that for the time being). Over five years, the government's outlay would total up to Rs 99,125 crore or nearly Rs one lakh crore on account of MPLADS.

Individual MPs are not accountable to anyone regarding what they have done with their Rs 25 crore during their terms. There is no audit at all. At its most practical, it is money for jam. Often it remains unspent. It was introduced by Prime Minister Narasimha Rao, in my view to keep MPs happy as his Congress government was some 50 MPs short of a majority. The figure then was Rs 2 crore annually. Dr Manmohan Singh increased the figure to Rs 5 crore, again to keep the MPs happier. In both cases, this scheme was a *baksheesh* to every MP—in exchange of support, present or future, to the government.

Rather than comment on this, let me give my own experience of the Rs 4 crore allotted to me for my two-year membership. My party allocated to me Vadodara, the city as well as the district. We are talking of the period towards the end of 2000. The party held a meeting of local workers of whom some 30 turned up. They warmly applauded my coming and garlanded me. I had never before been so honoured. In my brief speech, I thanked them but asked jocularly whether their warmth was out of regard for me or in expectation of our spending Rs 4 crore. The audience laughed, which eloquently meant the latter. I said we would meet again to decide what development works we should do and where.

The next day I went to see the District Collector who was warm and friendly. My request to him was to help me to implement this scheme as I had no machinery. I went to say that I did not wish to mix it up with my business. His advice was that I should set up an NGO and get the scheme implemented through it. Another wise man I consulted advised me to get my party MLAs together with a few active workers, and then verbally distribute the total fund amongst them. That meant that if an MLA was to get Rs 20 lakh, whatever work he recommended in his constituency, I would sign on. He would do the rest. I would ask no questions except go to inaugurate his works if he invited me. The wise man went on to say, "Then you see how these people work for you at election time in case you contest for the Lok Sabha next time."

Meanwhile, some non-political person suggested that

I should build as many Sulabh Shauchalayas as possible on Vadodara's streets. The common people, especially the women, would bless me. This suggestion not only gave me confidence but also a reliable, known and professional implementer. It took two odd years to get all the pieces of land also for ten bus stops in the city. In the rural sector, 88 brick and mortar bus stops were built, fortunately helped by the same agency. Medical equipment for Ahmedabad's public hospital Sheth Vadilal Sarabhai, a computer system in a school in Vadodara city and several *anganwadis* in a few villages too were set up. Imagine the amount of work that could be done with a mere Rs 4 crore!

In many cases, the MP finds it difficult to implement projects. In my time no particular item could entail more than Rs 10 lakhs. This meant that I had to spend my total grant on at least 40 small projects. Therefore, some MPs have a go at a few projects and leave the remaining funds unspent. Some distribute the money among local MLAs while others use the money for their own NGOs. The whole scheme is so clumsy that it is wasteful. It would have been useful if the purpose was only to distribute perquisites to Members of Parliament.

In spite of these shortcomings, if there be a parliamentary consensus for resuming the grants to MPs, let it be so. But a change in procedure is necessary. Let a keen MP apply to the Finance Minister stating what he/she proposes to do and within how much time. If an earmarked joint secretary finds the proposal viable and useful for the particular area, an approval could be given but subject to audit by a licenced auditor empanelled for MPLADS. The result would be beneficial to the area people, executed economically and with a degree of uprightness.

Gujarat and Change

India's ancient wisdom lay in distributing duties to Brahma, Vishnu and Mahesh—the Creator, the Preserver and the Destroyer, when necessary. No one deity can handle everything, no matter how powerful or versatile he is. But our people expect one minister or chief minister to win elections, run the government, supervise ministers, keep a tab over all MLAs and then win the elections again. In Gujarat's case, the then chief minister was not credited with winning the 2017 poll. It was won on the strength of Prime Minister Modi's popularity. It is an old belief that once elected the chief minister should carry on until the next poll, normally five years.

There is a firm impression among the political class that it was Bhupendrabhai Patel whose small company built the Sabarmati River Front which helped boost the beauty of Ahmedabad. The other impression is that he also constructed Ahmedabad's Bus Rapid Transit System, which is running successfully, unlike other cities where such a scheme did not take off. Since these achievements, Bhupendrabhai has been on the BJP's mind which likes modern schemes delivered in perfection and on time. He is a Kadva Patel, not a Leuva. They are supposed have descended from Rama's sons Lav and Kush; hence their names begin with L and K.

Another unnoticed factor is opportunity. Most MLAs, (182 in Gujarat), contest elections in the hope of becoming ministers of the government if they win, provided they belong to the winning party. Those who don't, generally have to shelve their hopes unless and until there is floor crossing on a big scale. If the party with a majority has say, a hundred seats, 25 might get a portfolio each. What about the remaining 75? They don't have much opportunity of self-promotion except the odd MLA, who might rise by chance. It is, therefore, appropriate that the party in power should make changes as the government moves along. Not all ministers are efficient and, therefore, need to be replaced.

In the peculiar Indian situation most parties need to replace an OBC with an OBC. The quality of his/her work is then usually sidelined. However, times are changing; today's youth do not give priority to caste as did their fathers or grandfathers. The youth of today want to get on in life. There is only a limited chance of this happening if the society or economy does not move on. That means qualitative development and quantitative growth of professions. They realise that they cannot expect development when the country's politics is hamstrung by caste. If politics does not change, there will be no progressive economy, only a static society—a recipe for misery. In short, if the leader of the party trying to win an election cannot promise development but only a status quo, the other party might win by default.

It is notable that Gujarat has not thrown up a third party—there are only the Congress and the BJP. All those who tried to be a third force have failed. The last to experiment with a third party was Keshubhai Patel, Gujarat's former (now deceased) chief minister. However, the only one elected from this new party was Keshubhai himself. In the coming assembly poll, there will be three parties contesting. Apart from the BJP and the Congress, the Aam Aadmi Party will also be contesting. The triangular contest should make things easier for BJP.

Gujarat is one state where economics subordinates politics. But the Congress, especially when Madhav Singh Solanki was chief minister, escalated casteism to extraordinary heights, a strategy borrowed from UP and Bihar. This wrote the script for the Congress' decline in Gujarat. For some elections, the party fought on a combination of castes called KHAM or Kshatriyas, Harijans, Adivasis and Muslims. The other mistake the Congress made was its socialism which is totally at odds with the Gujarati psyche. A Gujarati is sold on business and free enterprise. The Congress party remained in power for years only because there was none other.

Remarkably, Gujarat's tallest leaders have devoted themselves to the service of the country rather than confine themselves to their state. Swami Dayanand Saraswati founded the Arya Samaj movement as well as revived the Vedic practice of *shuddhi* or return to Hinduism voluntarily. Gandhi was never a state leader although he began his politics from the Kochrab Ashram in Ahmedabad. Sardar Patel worked for India phenomenally and unified the country following Independence, when two-fifths of it comprised princely states. Now we have

PM Modi, about whom volumes have been written and will continue to be written.

But the change of guard in Gujarat, as in Assam a few months ago, does demonstrate that the BJP does not shy away from making decisions for upgrading the polity. In pursuit of this goal, the party is least hesitant to replace incumbents. In complete contrast stands the Congress, which has been reduced to a family business, where only fawning courtiers are tolerated. The recent resignation of Captain Amarinder Singh, barely four months away from the Punjab assembly elections, says it all. His humiliation at the hands of Congress newcomers speaks volumes of how a once grand party now lives on a glory that has long vanished.

Ideology

It is essential for every political party to be wedded to an ideology, a comprehensive belief to hold it together. There are times when the party may be in opposition when the leaders have few fish and loaves of power to distribute to its members and cadres. Even when in government, not every member can be included among the beneficiaries. In all such eventualities, an ideology acts as a binding or uniting factor.

The Congress is a useful example to illustrate this phenomenon. It was founded in 1885 to enable leading Indians to voice their grievances. Then emerged Mohandas Karamchand Gandhi. By 1919-1920, he was espousing the cause of saving the throne of the medieval Sultan of Turkey who lost it in World War I, and of retaining his title as the Caliph of all Sunni Islam. Caliphate in Arabic is Khilafat and, therefore, this movement was named the Khilafat movement. Gandhi and his colleagues, the Ali brothers, considered religion as an attraction superior to a civilian emperor.

Gandhi soon gave a call for Non-cooperation with the British government to awaken Indians to the value of freedom. Soon enough, a police station at Chauri Chaura was set on fire by some violent agitators.

While the British ruled, the Congress did not need any ideology. The party was free to respond to all calls of British provocation, until they left India in 1947. The question of ideology should have arisen after that but the party made do instead with programmes like the 'socialistic pattern of society' which it coined at Avadi in 1955—Panchsheel, Non-alignment, and Indira Gandhi's 20 Point Programme. In the bargain, the ship of Congress had no compass and it lost its way.

An ideology should preferably be indigenous and not foreign. Surprisingly, many political parties follow ideologies of foreign origin. The new idea called Marxism gave birth to a new Russian empire in 1917 and misled it to its breakup and demise by 1991. The core of Marxism, contained in *Das Kapital,* was largely written in the British Museum and parts of it in Europe; its formation had nothing to do with Russia. In fact, Karl Marx had contended that a large and strong proletariat was necessary to engineer a workers' revolution. Russia had a very small working class and a large peasantry living in villages with fears that the communists would collectivise their land.

China also took to a communist path. But neither Germany nor Britain, advanced capitalist societies by at least Marx's standards, went communist. During the regime of Adolf Hitler, Germany adopted Fascism as its ideology; it was innovated in Italy. Fascism represents class collaboration rather than the class exploitation of capitalism and class conflict of communism.

The USA has two parties. The Republicans are more capitalist and the Democrats less so, rather like Britain's Liberals. The Scandinavian countries practise socialism or welfarism. In India, we are supposed to be practising 'dynamic socialism' in Nehru's words. It is only since 2014 that India is practising its own indigenous ideology, namely Hindu nationalism. Call it Hindudom if you like. Its emphasis is on dharma. It is not that India has abandoned the rule of law; it still prevails. Rule of dharma has an ethical element in it; it is defined at length in the *Bhagavad Gita* by Krishna. Veer Savarkar added to the concept. The latest effort is in a volume called *The Grammar of Hindudom*.

An Indian can grasp the ideas native to the land he lives on, but ask an Indian to understand Marxism and it would be tough going because its very ideas are foreign. The great Dr Ambedkar decided that he would not die a Hindu; but which faith to convert to? He rejected Islam and Christianity because he felt that they would be denationalising, as they were founded in West Asia, very far away from India.

After much thought and consultation, the learned doctor opted for Buddhism, primarily because it was first preached in India. Its founder Gautam Buddha is believed to be the ninth avatar of Vishnu. The message of Buddhism would be easy to understand by most common folk in India. Dr Ambedkar died a Buddhist.

For an election, when a candidate for a constituency is selected, the first question every political party raises is whether he belongs to the voting area—whether the voters can relate to him/her immediately, and equally, if he/she can relate to the voters. A candidate from another province would take a long time to get familiar with the constituency. Naveen Patnaik may or may not address his people in Odiya but he belongs to Odisha and everyone knows it. A Bengali who has grown up in Bhubaneswar would not have the same effect. What is true of a candidate should be true of an ideology as well.

Kashmir

A Kashmiri acquaintance recently described the situation in Kashmir as a continuation of the Indo-Pak conflict by proxy. Some locals fear that their Valley will soon be filled with outsiders, whereas more strident Kashmiris look at the abolition of Article 370 as an opportunity to prolong the fight.

Maulana Abdul Kalam Azad firmly opposed the partition of India. In 1983, a Pakistani journalist visited Tehran to interview Iran's religious dictator Ayatollah Khomeini, in connection with the celebrations around Pakistan Day, namely 23 March. The interviewer's final question was: What did Khomeini *sahib* think of Qaid-e-Azam Jinnah? The Ayatollah's answer was: He was a brilliant man but could have benefitted from his vision. He should have been patient and his community would have gotten the whole of India, not merely its crumbs. But then, Jinnah was not a *momin* but a recently-minted coin.

It is true that until 1935, Jinnah was widely called "the ambassador of Hindu-Muslim unity", a term coined by Sarojini

Naidu. In his presidential address on the eve of proposing the Pakistan Resolution in 1940, Jinnah said, "We know that the history of the last 1,200 years has failed to achieve unity and has witnessed India always divided into Hindu India and Muslim India. Muslim India cannot accept any constitution which must result in a Hindu majority government; in combination with democracy, it would be a Hindu raj which Muslims cannot tolerate".

The Qaid's other contention was that "Muslims are not a minority. Muslims are a nation according to any definition; they must have their homeland, their territory and their state".

Dr BR Ambedkar wrote in his 1941 reply to Jinnah's resolution: 'No one has expressed shock at the thought of separating Karnataka from Andhra, then what is there to be shocked at in the demand for the separation of Pakistan? If it is disruptive in its effect, it is no more so than the separation of Hindu provinces such as Karnataka from Maharashtra, or Andhra from Madras. Pakistan is merely another manifestation of a cultural unit demanding freedom. There is nothing new about the resolution which merely resuscitates the scheme which was put forth by Muhammad Iqbal in 1930. Mr Rahmat Ali gave it the name Pakistan. After Iqbal, there is nothing new in linking the north-western provinces'. There is nothing new in combining together the districts of Bengal and Assam into one province. Viceroy Curzon had done it in 1905. French Orientalist Joseph Renan has written that a nation is a living soul, a spiritual principle. 'The Hindus draw their inspiration from the Ramayana etc. whereas the Muslims derive their inspiration from the Quran and Hadith'. Thus, in Ambedkar's opinion, there was no argument against the claim for Partition.

Ambedkar quotes Lord Acton's phrase that Pakistan is 'a soul wandering in search of a body'. Ambedkar went deep into the subject and showed that the Indian army then was dominated in numbers by Muslim Punjabis, but their pay and perks were indirectly paid for by the Hindu provinces. He concluded by writing that in any case it was better to have the enemy outside the borders rather than inside.

To go back to the Kashmir issue, could it be that the government in Delhi and the governor in Srinagar are unable to relate to the Kashmiris who are of a different faith? They begin with God, move on to the Prophet and then to the scripture. On the other hand, we do not have a single authoritative book or Prophet but are believers in karma. Their way of thinking, in the lingo of logic is called deductive, which begins with a premise and ends with a logical conclusion, top down. Our faith is inductive and begins with ground realities to move upwards till it reaches a conclusion. A few scholars realise the huge gulf between the two categories of faiths, Abrahamic and Eastern.

The Abrahamic method of approaching the issue would be to shoot and kill, whereas the Eastern way would be to worry about the relationship between the two sides after the bullets and battles. This explains how we are an ancient civilization and at the same time, have taken nearly 75 years to get down to grappling with the problem.

India and Pakistan were born as independent countries at the same time. Yet look at the difference in the distance covered by the two countries. To overcome the gulf in the Kashmir Valley, everyone should understand one another so that the Government of India does not keep going 'round and round the mulberry bush'.

IMDT Act, 1983

The Illegal Migrants (Determination by Tribunals) IMDT Act, 1983, is legislation by the Indian Parliament to identify Bangladeshi infiltrators. Amazingly, the Act applies only to the State of Assam. Even the immediate neighbouring states like Meghalaya are not covered. In fact, the rest of India works under the Foreigners Act, 1946, and the Citizenship Act, 1955.

Under sub section (I) of Section 8 of the Act of 1983, any person may make an application to the tribunal for its decision whether the person whose name and other particulars are given in the application is or is not an illegal immigrant. However, for making such an application, it is conditional that the person/illegal migrant in relation to whom the application is made must reside within 3 km from the place of residence of the applicant. Otherwise, the Tribunal shall not entertain the application.

One stringent condition has been stipulated in the Act of 1983 which provides that the application to be made in the prescribed form shall be accompanied by an affidavit sworn by not less than two persons residing within 3 km of the area in which the person against whom the complaint is made is found or residing, corroborating the averments made in the application.

Another outstanding feature of the Act is that the burden of proving that a person is a foreigner is on the applicant who complains that a particular person is an illegal migrant. The Foreigners Act, 1946, which applies to the rest of India, places the burden of proving a person to be a citizen of India and not an illegal migrant on the suspect.

On receipt of an application under sub section (2) of Section 8, the Tribunal shall issue a notice, accompanied by a copy of the application, to the prescribed authority calling upon it to furnish, after making such inquiry as that authority may deem fit, a report to the Tribunal with regard to the averments made in the application. If on a consideration of the report made by the prescribed authority the Tribunal is satisfied that:

(a) The person named in the application is not an illegal migrant or that the application is frivolous or has not been made in good faith, the Tribunal shall, after giving the applicant an opportunity to be heard, reject the application.

(b) There are reasonable grounds to believe that the person named in the application is an illegal migrant, the Tribunal shall issue a notice accompanied by a copy of the application to the person named in the application, calling upon him to make, within thirty days from the date of receipt of the notice, such representation with regard to the averments made in the application and to produce such evidence as he may think fit in support of his defence.

If the Tribunal is satisfied that the person aforesaid was prevented by sufficient cause from making his presentation and from producing evidence in support of his defence within the period of thirty days, it may permit him to make his representation and to produce evidence in support of his defence, within such further period, not exceeding thirty days, as it may by order specify.

How stringent is the procedure prescribed by IMDT in order to judge a suspect to be an illegal migrant is evident. But not merely that, there is a provision for two layers of appeal beyond the judgment of the tribunal, namely the Appellant Tribunal as well as the High Court. This makes it well-nigh impossible to declare anyone an illegal migrant.

The IMDT Act was made into law by the Congress government in 1983. Its single aim was to placate the minority sentiments, which welcome infiltration from Bangladesh in order to increase the Muslim population of the state of Assam.

Grand Old Prejudice

Former Assam Chief Minister Tarun Gogoi's opposition to the proposed repeal of the IMDT Act may seem a betrayal of those young Assamese men and women who laid down their lives in the anti-infiltration cause. The movement began in 1979 at Mangaldai, Begam Anwara Taimur's constituency. The day the Congress, which India's media calls the "grand old party", flayed the centre for its proposed repeal was the same when Parliament passed an amendment to the Foreigners Act, which has been the law in every state barring Assam since 1946.

The main difference between the two laws is that, under the Foreigner's Act, the onus of proving one's Indian citizenship lies with the suspect. This is about the same as laws prevailing in most countries. The IMDT stands out like a sore thumb, because it places the onus of proving before a special tribunal that a person is not a citizen on the complainant who should reside within three km of the suspect's residence. The threat of being harmed or killed is itself a deterrent for the complainant, not to speak of nailing an illegal migrant. The IMDT seems to ensure that infiltrators are not detected and certainly not evicted. For the Congress to oppose the repeal of such an anti-national law is indeed unfortunate.

Evidently, the party is at sixes and sevens to respond to forces like the VHP (Vishwa Hindu Parishad). In the Gujarat Assembly polls in December 2017, it adopted soft Hindutva and was described by the media as the BJP's 'B' team. Both Shankar Singh Vaghela and Sonia Gandhi began their campaigns by visiting temples. It was hard to find a Congress candidate not flaunting a big red *tika* on his forehead.

In Madhya Pradesh, the state's former (Congress) Chief Minister Digvijay Singh had fumbled on the Dhar Bhojshala. Eventually, he had to open the temple for a whole day every week instead of one day every year. The credit for the concession to Hindus went to the Centre. In Rajasthan, the Congress regime has, by opposing *trishul diksha* and arresting Pravin Togadia, made the VHP prominent. In Delhi, it would have done the same thing but luckily for the party, law and order in the Capital is a Central subject.

Sonia Gandhi's opposition to the IMDT's repeal is not the Congress's first pro-Muslim gesture. Years ago in 1986, the then prime minister Rajiv Gandhi had overturned the Supreme Court judgement in the Shah Bano case by using his party's brute majority in Parliament to pass the Muslim Women's Bill. Indira Gandhi was no different. In 1967, a five-member Bench of the apex court had held that the Aligarh Muslim University was not a Muslim minority institution. It was established and administered by the Government in pursuance of the 1920 Act. Indira Gandhi had this ruling overturned by an Act of Parliament.

Nehru was once described by a wag as "the only nationalist Muslim in India". His 'achievements' were Articles 29 and 30, which provided the minorities with special privileges. These had been offered in 1946 in an attempt to dissuade Muslims from insisting on Partition. Even after India was divided, riots took place and people were butchered, but Nehru did nothing to scrap these Articles.

A few months before he was assassinated, Mahatma Gandhi fasted to force the Government of India to pay Rs 55 crores to Pakistan, as part of the Partition agreement, even though that country had still not halted its genocide of Hindus. Gandhi had launched his political career in India by leading the Khilafat Movement to demand the restoration of the Turkish Sultan, who had till 1918, also been the Caliph of the faith. Such a cause had nothing to do with India. The Congress's pro-Muslim tradition was begun by its then President, Badruddin Tyabji in 1888. To quote him: 'The Congress could only deal with matters in which Mussalmans as a community were not opposed and would only deal with matters in which they agreed'.

India is only Half-Sovereign

The US declaration of Independence in 1776 was the first document to enunciate sovereignty as an essential element of the new state. The French Constitution of 1797 stated: 'Sovereignty is one, indivisible, unalienable and imprescriptible; it belongs to the nation: no group can attribute sovereignty to itself nor can an individual arrogate it to himself'. The concept was first thought of by Jean Bodin of 16th century France to signal the progress from feudalism to nationalism.

The June 2010 incident of two Naga groups—ANSAM (All India Naga Students' Association) and NSF (Naga Students' Federation)—blockading Manipur by choking NH-39 and NH-53 in the State is reminiscent of a siege undertaken in war. Instead of calling in the army to disperse the involved groups and restoring the normal passages to and fro Manipur, the government airlifted supplies. Home Secretary VK Duggal is reported (*The Statesman*, 18 August 2010) to have said in Manipur on 17 August that it was the state's 'internal' matter.

This was rather like the US Air Force reaching West Berlin in 1961 when the Soviet Union had blockaded the city. In this incident, three independent countries were involved—Federal Republic of Germany, the US and the USSR. In the Naga-Manipur episode only one country—and therefore a domestic problem—was there.

On Independence Day in 2005, the Naxalites killed persons including an Andhra Pradesh MLA C Narsi Reddy. Andhra Pradesh is not the only state infested with extremists. In the last week of July that year, seven people were killed in Bastar and Chhattisgarh by Maoists. The insurgency rose steadily over the decade of the 1990s and by the 2000s, some 200 districts of the country were affected. In a number of them, even the police had no easy entry to the sub-divisional towns. Yet, the Central Government's panel in those years appointed to review cases booked under POTA accused the Andhra Pradesh police of 'misusing' the law.

Ms Mamata Banerjee, currently West Bengal's chief minister, when she was a Member of Parliament earlier, on one occasion in August 2005 threw a sheaf of papers at the Deputy Speaker of the Lok Sabha. The reason was her protest at the way delimitation of constituencies was taking place in West Bengal. In a number of constituencies, she had discovered Bangladeshi nationals listed in Indian rolls. It is amazing that foreigners were being enabled to vote in our elections.

What is happening in West Bengal is not accidental as it has been the policy of the Congress and the Leftist parties to encourage infiltration and thus expand their vote-bank. Had it not been so, how can the Congress party explain its sponsorship of the IMDT Act in Assam and its unhappiness at its having been struck down as ultravires by the Supreme Court?

When in April 2005, Maulana Asad Madani pleaded for more privileges for Muslims, the then Assam Chief Minister Tarun Gogoi had pointed out at the Congress's support for the IMDT Act. Assam was the only state where this law was in force. It was also unique in the world because nowhere did the law place the onus of proving that a suspected infiltrator is really so on the complainant. The alleged person has no responsibility to prove his bona fides. The Left Front, which was then ruling in West Bengal, had said that it was a 'desirable' law and should also be introduced in West Bengal.

India's policy with regard to Jammu & Kashmir till the year 2014 was equally amazing. Years ago, Parliament had resolved that the whole of Jammu & Kashmir is an integral and unalienable part of India, which included Pakistan-occupied Kashmir (PoK). Yet Article 370 of the Constitution continued to prevail until our current Prime Minister Narendra Modi in one stroke terminated it in 2019. The state even had a separate Constitution. A Kashmiri could freely buy property in any part of the country, but non-Kashmiri Indians could not acquire anything in Jammu & Kashmir. Yet, previous governments expected people to believe that we were a sovereign state.

Meanwhile, those erstwhile governments experienced no embarrassment in negotiating autonomy in Jammu & Kashmir with all and sundry, including the various factions of the Hurriyat who are nothing but separatists. The Government of India did not mind the Hurriyat leaders from hobnobbing with Pakistani diplomats or with visiting dignitaries from Islamabad. Equally incorrigible was the spectacle of the previous governments holding talks at home as well as overseas with Naga separatists like T Muivah. A sovereign state would charge every separatist with treason, try him and hang him if proved guilty.

This is clear from the fact that the *wakf* properties represent the biggest urban landlords in India. The demand for Taj Mahal by the Sunni Wakf Board and for Bibi ka Maqbara at Aurangabad by the Maharashtra Wakf Board is on the grounds that these contain *qabrs* (graves). A sovereign state should nationalise all their properties as they are deemed to belong to Allah who is supreme and much above any country or its laws.

Similarly, Muslim personal laws still continue to be sacred and above the purview of the Constitution. Contrary to the Supreme Court's view, the Muslim community now even argues vociferously for setting up Sharia courts known as Dar-ul-Qaza in a number of states to adjudicate on matters concerning marriage, divorce, etc. This is nothing but a demand to recognise two systems of law and justice in the country—one Muslim and the other Indian. In the event there is a conflict between the two, the Muslim version is supposed to prevail.

The evident conclusion would be that India is a half-sovereign state. This concept was articulated by the German jurist on International Law, JJ Moser, who lived in the 18th century. India has some attributes of sovereignty like its belonging to the nation and not to any individual; it being also imprescriptible. But between the Sharia and *Wakf*, sovereignty is shared and not absolute. Negotiations with Kashmiri and Naga separatists earlier have been an indication that it is neither indivisible nor inalienable.

Mockery at Bhojshala

The conflict at Bhojshala in Dhar, as reported by *The Pioneer* (3 February 2012), brought back for me an unfortunate memory. It was a morning in the winter of 1999 when accompanied by my colleagues I reached Dhar. One obvious place to stop was the Bhojshala. To my surprise and disappointment, I was told by the Central Reserve Policemen at the gate that I could not enter this temple built by Raja Bhoj because it had since been converted into Kamal Maula Masjid.

I appealed to the police inspector that I had a right to enter this place of worship; for his safety, I assured him that I was a Member of Parliament. He then asked me to go to the Collector's office and get the permission. His plea was that since the Muslim sentiment was a sensitive issue, he could not take any risk of letting me in except at the risk of losing his job. To console me, he said that any Hindu could come back on Basant Panchami and Muslims could go for up to two hours on Friday. What hurt me was that in a temple a Hindu could go only once a year, whereas Muslims, who had usurped the holy place, could visit it every week. It was an eloquent commentary on Indian secularism.

This blatantly discriminatory order was issued by the Digvijay Singh government in 1997, when reports said that there was some Hindu-Muslim tension in the area. The excuse given was that Bhojshala was, in any case, a protected monument and barricading it would be the best way to secure its protection. Incidentally, there was no threat from anyone either damaging or demolishing the structure. The discriminatory order of entry 52 times a year to one community and only once a year to another is based on an extraordinary precedent.

I understand that in 1935, on the insistence of some local residents of Dhar, which was then a princely state, Bhojshala was a Hindu institution—the temple of Goddess Saraswati on the one hand, and a school on the other. Its idol is still on display in the British Museum in London. A part of the Sanskrit inscription which is engraved on a wall of Bhojshala is also reproduced. It is called *Dhar Prasasti of Arjunvarm: parijatamanjari-natika* by Madana.

On the strength of their conviction, the local residents demanded that the Bhojshala mosque be reconverted into a temple. Although the Maharaja of Dhar was a Hindu, he was under the influence of the British Resident who was reported to have advised him to ban entry into the edifice for a while. The Maharaja, therefore, did as advised, except for allowing Hindus to enter on Basant Panchami day, which is the day of Saraswati Puja. Similarly, Muslims were allowed entry on one day in the year. This precedent was twisted by the Digvijay Singh regime into a discriminatory order mentioned earlier.

Such are the wages of secularism in India.

It is best to quote the letter dated 1 May 1952 issued by the collector of Dhar of the then Madhya Bharat state, which later became a part of Madhya Pradesh. "I am directed to request you to kindly to inform the Hindu Mahasabha that the building called Bhojshala situated at Dhar cannot be given to either the Hindu or the Muslim communities for conversion into a temple or a mosque and that this being an archaeological monument, the right of entry to it would be conceded to all sections of people for purpose of sightseeing. The Muslim community may also be kindly informed, if necessary, that while Muslims may continue to say their Friday prayers in the building, no effects must be kept there and nobody should use any part of it for residence" (The Dhar State Huzur Durbar office file year 1935-36).

Bhojshala was a college. *The District Gazetteer* says that Raja Bhoj School is a mosque, a part of which was converted from a Hindu institution of the 11th century, the Saraswati temple or school. According to the publication, this shrine of Saraswati, the Hindu goddess of learning, is described in the Sanskrit play of Arjunvarma Paramara (1210-16). Two slabs were discovered behind the *mehrab*, one bearing the Prakrit odes of the 11th century (supposed to have been composed by Raja Bhoj himself) and the other the Sanskrit play mentioned above, which praises Arjunvarma. These slabs stand on the north side of the building and are beautiful specimens of the stonecutter's work.

The Department of Archaeology, Gwalior, 1952, has in a special book dealt with the cultural heritage of Madhya Bharat, which, in 1956, amalgamated with the Central Provinces and came to be known as Madhya Pradesh. This book, *Dhar and Mandu*, reiterates what Major CE Luard, the official gazetteer of Dhar had said in 1912. The carved pillars used all over the building and the delicately carved ceilings of the prayer hall seem to have belonged to the original Bhojshala.

On the pavement of the prayer hall are seen numerous slabs of black slate stone, the writings on which were also scraped off. From a few slabs recovered from another part of the building and now exhibited there, which contain the texts of the poetic works of *Parijatamanjari* and *Kurmastotra*, it appears that the old college was adorned with numerous Sanskrit and Maharashtri Prakrit texts, beautifully engraved on such slabs.

Only Governance Matters

Some time ago the Union Home Ministry informed Parliament that it has received recommendations from the public for the creation of several new states. Although no state government has made a suggestion, the proposals range from Bhojpur, Coorg, Gorkhaland, Koshalanchal to Mithilanchal. Many of these recommendations are frivolous but they do reflect discontent over the declining quality of governance. When the Bihar fodder scam was big news, it was not crucial whether the chief minister had pocketed Rs 600 crore or more. What was important was that he had failed to govern. This is not to say that his predecessors were much better administrators. Governments in Patna have generally been poor and unstable since the general elections of 1967.

There is a connection between this failure and the unfortunate popularity of politicians like Raj Thackeray in Mumbai in recent years. In this regard, UP is a bigger bird of the same feather. The residents of the two states have been steadily migrating to other states for employment even if it be at below subsistence wage; which, in turn, sharply undercuts the local workmen. This is sad when one notes that most of the paragraphs of Chapter VII of the States Reorganization Commission Report (SRC) 1955, speak about the Five Year Plan and the effect of the size of the state on development. Since Independence, we were all concerned about poverty in India regardless of how much we were able to reduce it. But since the slogan of 'India Shining' was launched, even this concern has been pushed to the backburner. Meanwhile, other than the urban middle and upper classes, most people are marking time or getting poorer. In any case, the contrast between the common man's plight and the upwardly mobile Indian has become painfully sharp. Television only serves to exaggerate the differences. Thackeray is not the only rabble-rouser who is cashing in on the resulting discontent. The Maoists are much greater and wider beneficiaries of the 'Groaning India'.

The contrast between the rich and the poor is not confined to urban and rural or between the professionals and the non-educated. It is equally sharp between region and region, state and state. If the country were to be segregated into five regions, the east and the central are languishing. The north, comprising Punjab, Haryana and Delhi, the west and the south are flourishing. People from Bihar and UP who go to Mumbai, Delhi or cities in Gujarat, do so because they are desperate for employment. Many of them work for a pittance. The desperation is such that Brahmins from Bihar are seen tending and cleaning Sulabh *shauchalayas* (toilets) in cities like Vadodara.

With the passage of time, the freedom struggle and all that patriotic fervour it aroused has receded into distant memory.

Globalisation and free trade are taking a toll of nationalism; so are the increasing consumerism and the lure of earning money. The youth of tomorrow may well become self-centred enough to ignore the importance of national integrity. A time may come, several decades hence, when the youth of a prosperous state can question the need to pay for carrying the burden of backward states as parts of their country. It is noteworthy that states that are officially declared backward get central subsidies through the Finance Commission for not being able to raise taxes sufficient to meet their essential revenue expenditure. Youth from a more affluent state can question the need of their state to pay for the inefficiency of regimes that leech off the supposedly backward states.

The questioning youth, in his misguided intolerance, may cite the example of the Soviet Union which spontaneously decided to allow its 14 republics or provinces to go their separate ways. Yugoslavia was yet another unfortunate case of provinces seceding one by one; beginning with Slovenia followed by Croatia, Bosnia Herzegovina, Macedonia and later, part of the province of Kosovo. Nationalism can no longer be taken for granted as a safeguard of a country's unity. Until the 18th century, religion was the ideology which supported the monarchs of Europe. Thereafter, nationalism became the binding factor of European countries.

In contrast, communism considered the nation-state an instrument of exploitation of the poor in the hands of the rich. It exhorted the workers of the world to unite. Internationalism became its slogan. India has plenty of communists. It also has many *ulema* whose commitment is to the world *ummah* in preference to any loyalty to the country. The nation-state has no place in Islamic ideology; nor do national frontiers matter to them. The confusion is confounded worse by the fact of Pakistan and Bangladesh being neighbours. The safeguards of national integrity, therefore, are fewer in India than say, in the USA, Japan or even the formerly communist China which has 93 percent people belonging to the Han race.

Indians have to be more careful in their endeavour to remain a united country. They should not, as some of its elitists do, dream of the European Union which has now one currency, one visa and so on. Loose talk about a confederation of south Asian countries would only dilute the focus on Indian unity. In the ultimate analysis, advice like this would have limited value. The main responsibility would be on how our states provide a structural balance to the Indian federation. No state should be too large or dominant due to its big population.

Family planning should provide an essential curb on the proliferation of numbers, irrespective of the community. On the other hand, no state should be so small as to be economically unviable. The central doles to states should be minimised; certainly UP and Bihar should help to create surpluses rather than deficits, so that rabble-rousers like Raj Thackeray should not get any opportunity. Uneven growth and prosperity does cause inter-state envy and tension. In other words, if another SRC is appointed, its primary duty would be to redesign such a federal map that the states would lend themselves to efficient governance. As the future unfolds, language, caste and even religion are likely to decline in importance. Economic efficiency would be the key to the national integrity of India.

Disempowerment
of a Majority

Ms Radha Rajan, a journalist and author, had some time ago written on Gandhi as the 'hero' of the eclipse of the Hindu *rashtra*. She wrote her eponymous book during the period when Dr Manmohan Singh occupied the seat of India's prime minister. Dr Singh earned considerable notoriety for publicly saying that "Muslims must have the first claim on India's resources", for which he earned opprobrium. But Ms Rajan's book was an act of courage; in fact, extraordinary courage when one bears in mind that secular fundamentalism has been the order, nay the mania, of the last century. In 1919, Gandhi put his stamp on this fundamentalism that would follow by presiding over the Khilafat Movement for restoring the deposed Sultan of Turkey as the Caliph of all Islam. Even Muhammad Ali Jinnah had opposed the Khilafat Movement. Who could help the Hindus when their supremo for the next three decades was more pro-Islamic than the founder of the Muslim homeland? We quote some sentences which highlight

Ms Rajan's thesis on the Hindu eclipse:

This work attempts to trace the origins and the trajectory of Indian polity over the last 130 years, culminating in the de-Hinduisation of the polity and political disempowering of the Hindus. Gandhi stepped into a vacuum created by Aurobindo's abdication of political responsibility....

The end of colonial rule in 1947, while it ceded state power to the Hindus who then comprised 87.22% of the population did not, however, put in place a self-conscious Hindu state. Contrary to the conventions of world history, India alone, after a decisive end of Muslim and White Christian rule in 1947, failed to establish a state reflecting the religion, culture and civilisational ethos of its majority populace. This was also the religion and culture of the soil, adhered to by the native populace, unlike the situation in North America, Australia, New Zealand and Islamic countries, where all traces of pre-Islamic and pre-Christian faiths have been wiped out. Wherever pre-Christian and pre-Islamic faiths and people have managed to survive, their numbers are puny like the Native Americans in North and South America, the Maoris of New Zealand or the Aborigines of Australia, and pose no threat to the conquering religion or race, as their numbers are too insignificant to dislodge their tormentors.

In India alone, post-1947 a polity and state emerged, powered by what came to be called Nehruvian secularism, actively hostile to the majority populace, a state which effectively de-Hinduised all public spaces, de-Hinduised the content and character of the polity, and politically disempowered the Hindus. Nehruvian Secularism owed its existence to Gandhi and Nehru; the latter was Gandhi's endowment to the fledgling nation-state.

It is bitterly ironical that Gandhi inaugurated his political career by writing *Ram Raj*. He also wrote *Hind Swaraj* which Ms Rajan has called "Christian Ramrajya". She has reiterated how Gandhi helped along by Jawaharlal Nehru prevented the establishment of a Hindu rashtra despite the British handing over power to the Hindus on 15 August 1947 in New Delhi. It was a golden opportunity that came the Hindu way after centuries of alien rule, first Muslim and then British. Instead of empowering the Hindus, these Congress bigwigs did their best to obliterate their political identity. The British, with all their imperial designs, never questioned the Hindu identity, parallel with that of the Muslim. What the Gandhian legacy did was to sustain the Muslim identity in the garb of minority pandering and rubbed out the Hindu in the name of pluralism. By and large, the so-called minority demands were ensconced as fundamental rights while what were the special needs of the Hindus were enumerated as directive principles of policy which could stay unimplemented for an indefinite period of time. Even the uniform civil code, which is absolutely essential for one country, one law, and is required by Article 44, has not been put into practice.

With all his Hindu postures, prayers and bhajans, Gandhi ignored the elementary fact that for the Hindu, state power was more necessary than to the communities inspired by the Semitic religions, whether Judaism, Christianity or Islam. Apart from scriptures and guides to daily life, these religions are social ideologies with lslam being also a political manifesto.

Although only 15 percent of the Indian population, Muslims have retained their separate personal laws. No matter what the rest of the world says, a Muslim man can be polygamous and can divorce his wife on e-mail or even when drunk! The community spontaneously knows how to flex its muscles and wield power; state power is welcome but not essential for its well-being.

The Hindu is the virtual opposite. For example, even after so many years of BJP rule, Hindu middle-class families find it difficult to keep residing in Kalupur, Dariapur, Jamalpur and many other parts of the walled city of Ahmedabad. All that needs to happen is the acquisition of one or two flats by Muslim families in a mansion. Thereafter, all they need to do is to begin cooking fish or meat and the odours would make the Hindu neighbours uncomfortable. Before long, they would wish to sell out and move to vegetarian havens.

Over a period of time, many a locality gets emptied of Hindus and a few eventually become no-go areas where even the police cannot penetrate. These may seem relatively trivial factors but they constitute an assault on the sovereignty of the Indian state built, in the words of author Rajan, on the foundation of Nehruvian secularism. What she did not mention in her book is that an Islamic State was being raised on the Manmohan Singh "Muslims first"thinking, which is really the Nehruvian ideology.

Many wonder why Gandhi aggravated the Hindu agony instead of trying to help his community. Maybe he was so bitterly anti-British that getting rid of them was his overwhelming priority. It is useful to recall the several humiliations which he suffered at the hands of the rulers.

The first was at Rajkot, where young prince Bhavsingh had removed some state jewels from the treasury. The blame for the mischief fell on Gandhi's elder brother Laxmidas who was the chief minister of the small princely state. In his student days in London, Gandhi had met Charles Ollivant, who had since become the resident commissioner. In the belief that he could influence the gentleman in favour of his brother, he went to see him. The Englishman was so annoyed at Gandhi's extra-legal persistence that he called his doorkeeper and had Gandhi thrown out physically. The incident became common gossip in Rajkot within hours.

Yet another humiliation which is well-known was when Gandhi was thrown out of a train at a station Pietermaritzburg because he was a coloured Asian travelling by first class, which was presumably meant only for the whites.

Whether these were the causes or any other, the fact is that Gandhi's life mission was anti-British. It is doubtful that the great man had read much history. To that extent, his understanding of affairs was many a time simplistic. For example, since the British practised 'divide and rule', he thought he would 'unite and fight', which meant Hindu-Muslim unity at any cost. His first major act in achieving unity was to lead the Khilafat Movement, which he thought would appeal to all Muslims because it was a struggle to restore the deposed Sultan of Turkey as the Caliph. Muhammad Ali Jinnah, however, did not support the movement. The Ottoman Empire had fallen in World War I; the Sultan was exiled from Turkey and the Caliphate abolished in 1924.

How little Gandhi understood the Muslim mind was illustrated by Maulana Mohammad Ali, his right hand man in the Khilafat Movement who publicly stated: "However pure Mr Gandhi's character may be, he must appear to me from the point of view of religion inferior to any Mussalman, even though he be without character". Many were dumbstruck when they saw this statement published in the press; many others dismissed it as a press fabrication. And when, sometime later, Mohammed Ali happened to address a public meeting at Lucknow, a straight question was put to him, and he eloquently accepted the statement attributed to him saying, "Yes, according to my religion and creed, I do hold an adulterous and a fallen Mussalman to be better than Mr Gandhi".

Again, for example, Annie Besant, an Irish lady, former President of the Congress, condemned the Moplah riots of 1927 as utterly ghastly; 600 Hindus were killed and hundreds of women were raped while 2,500 were forcibly converted to Islam. "It would be well if Mr Gandhi could be taken into Malabar to see with his own eyes the ghastly horrors which have been created by the preaching of himself and his 'loved brothers' Mohammad and Shaukat Ali". Sir Sankaran Nair, member of the Viceroy's Council wrote: "For sheer brutality on women, I do not remember anything in history to match the Malabar rebellion". Gandhi's final comment on the Moplahs was that "the Muslims were merely following their religion".

During the Kohat riots many a Hindu was killed and many women were abducted. To Gandhi, the Muslims were justified whereas the Hindus of Kohat were cowards. Swami Shraddhananda, disciple of the great Swami Dayanand Saraswati, was murdered in his sickbed in 1926 by one Abdul Rashid, who was tried and hanged to death by a British court. Gandhi reacted by calling Rashid a 'brother'. He did not even regard him as guilty of the swami's murder. Despite a series of experiences which should have brought home the hostile relationship between the two communities, Gandhi refused to accept the reality. At the second Round Table Conference in 1931, he nonchalantly stated that Hindu-Muslim disputes were coeval with British rule. There were hardly any disputes before the British arrived and they would cease as soon as the British left.

Dr BR Ambedkar held a completely different opinion. He eloquently summed up the situation:

"Such is the record of Hindu-Muslim relationship from 1920 to1940. Placed side by side with the frantic efforts made by Mr Gandhi to bring about Hindu-Muslim unity, the record makes most painful and heartrending reading. It would not be much exaggeration to say that it is a record of twenty years of civil war between the Hindus and the Muslims in India, interrupted by brief intervals of armed peace".

The less Gandhi understood the Muslims and what they wanted, the more he exploited the Hindus because he knew them and their weaknesses like the back of his palm. To support not only Muslims but also Pakistan after Partition, he fasted and blackmailed the government of India into transferring Rs 55 crores to Karachi even though Pakistan had invaded Kashmir. To assuage his political frustration, he did not hesitate to politically eclipse the Hindus in their own country. This is Ms Radha Rajan's submission in her courageous book.

In a vicarious but forceful statement, Gandhi's third son Ramdas wrote: "Your life has become a curse for the Hindu *jati*". Chaudhry Khaliquzzaman, one of the leaders of the Muslim League asked Gandhi: "What do you propose to do about it?" The reply was: "I want to fight it out with my life. I would not allow the Mussalmans to crawl on the streets in India. They must walk with self-respect".

GLOBAL POLITICS

Russia and China

One is unable to understand the Russian regime's inability to realise that Russia's greatest enemy potentially would be China and certainly not the USA. Moscow's obsession with America earlier was due to its illusion that the Soviet Union was a superpower. In Josef Stalin's reckoning, it was primarily the USSR that was instrumental in the defeat of Nazi Germany in World War II. He overlooked that the USA and Britain were the Western front and a lot of his weaponry and other material had been supplied under the Lend Lease Act legislated by the USA. The Soviet Union was not a very strong European power before the war; its economy was neither resourceful nor efficient. It did not merit nurturing dreams of being a superpower, a dream that eventually resulted in the collapse of the Soviet Union itself. Stalin's delusion passed on to his successor Nikita Khrushchev, who in turn passed it on to Leonid Brezhnev. It was only Mikhail Gorbachev who could see the reality, by which time it was too late.

Comrade Putin appears to be making an equally dangerous mistake by ignoring the potential threat from China. He was only 17 years old in 1969 when the Soviet Union fought a seven-month long mini war across the Ussuri River, which is located in Russia's Siberia or 'sleeping land'. How big was Beijing's ambition one does not know, but the Soviets had to convey an implicit nuclear threat to the aggressor. To save his face, Mao Zedong, through his premier Zhou Enlai, threatened a "People's War", which meant that hundreds of thousands of Chinese soldiers would swarm Soviet tanks, as they had done with the Americans in the Korean War in 1951-52. The Chinese leader's belief of convenience was the superiority of man over machine. The People's Liberation Army (PLA) did demonstrate its idea of warfare on one of the islands on the Ussuri by ambushing Soviet soldiers.

In the end, China gained quite a few islands on the river, which was a loss for the Soviet Union. Logically, more conflict lies ahead. China is a much bigger nuclear power than it was in 1969. Its ambitions have grown and by the current indications, it wishes to become a superpower. We have to remember that Siberia is over 13 million square kilometres with a sparse population, whereas China is bubbling with people but is short of arable land. Incidentally, the yellow giant gained several hundred islands in the midst of not only the Ussuri but also the Amur and Argun rivers. This gain by China and loss by the USSR was after decades of harrowing negotiations which ended in 2004.

With the earth experiencing climate change and parts of it getting warmer, Siberia could well become more hospitable. Today, the whole region is considered hostile due to its very low temperatures in winter. It gets as cold as -25 degrees centigrade on an average; at its coldest, it touches -46 degrees centigrade. In other words, with global warming, Siberia, east of the Ural Mountains and stretching to Vladivostok on the Pacific Ocean, is likely to become attractive for China to occupy. Parts of Siberia are rich in minerals to add to its attractions. The region, called Sibir in Russian, is rich in coal, natural gas, diamonds, iron ore, gold and aluminium. The visionary Czar towards the end of the 16th century sent groups of Cossacks led by a heroic Yermak who occupied gradually the whole area now a part of Russia.

A possible scenario of China forcibly occupying Siberia can no longer be looked upon as hypothetical or imaginary. Patrick Prinston, a Western columnist informs us that a Chinese portal *Jinji Toutiao* published an article, the author of which calls Siberia "Chinese land". The Chinese media regularly praises Russian ruler Vladimir Putin for what he is and how cleverly he puts the West in its place. Simply put, from the point of view of Beijing, Russia is not only a good friend but also has an excellent potential prize. "There are no countries around the world that are always friendly, or conversely, always hostile to each other. In the past, Siberia was conquered by the Mongols and is, therefore, in fact, a Chinese territory". This is increasingly becoming China's refrain.

In recent months, one of the inhabitants of Siberia organised a collective boycott of China, collecting two hundred and fifty thousand signatures. He wants Russia to stop exporting timber to China within ten years. Siberian forests are of great value for Russia. However, following the sharp increase in the volume of foreign trade in recent years, the local forest has been cut down on a large scale.

Joe Burgess in his column in *The New York Times* "Why China Reclaims Siberia" (July 26, 2021) lays out an ever starker scenario: "A land without people for a people without land", Burgess says. At the turn of the 20th century, that slogan promoted Jewish migration to Palestine. It could be recycled today justifying a Chinese takeover of Siberia. The land is as resource-rich and people-poor as China is the opposite. The weight of that logic scares the Kremlin. A border is real only if both sides believe in it. And on both sides of the Sino-Russian border, that belief is wavering. Siberia—the Asian part of Russia, east of the Ural Mountains—is immense. It makes up three-quarters of Russia's land mass, the equivalent of the entire USA and India put together.

The 1.35 billion Chinese people south of the border outnumber Russia's 144 million almost 10 to 1. The discrepancy is even starker for Siberia, home to barely 38 million people, especially the border area where only 6 million Russians face over 90 million Chinese. With intermarriage, trade and investment across that border, Siberians have realised that, for better or for worse, Beijing is a lot closer than Moscow. The land is already providing China (the factory of the world), with much of its raw materials, especially oil, gas and timber. Increasingly, Chinese-owned factories in Siberia churn out finished goods, as if the region already were a part of the Middle Kingdom's economy. Beijing could use Russia's own strategy: hand out passports to sympathisers in contested areas, and then move in militarily to "protect its citizens". If Beijing chooses to take Siberia by force, the only way Moscow could stop it would be by using nuclear weapons.

In televised remarks during a virtual meeting with senior

officials on 20 May 2021, Russian President Vladimir Putin, using a bit of colourful language, threatened to "knock out the teeth" of anyone who tried to bite off even a piece of Siberia. He surely could not have been thinking of the USA or the West. Chinese dictator Xi Jinping only last year described Putin as his "best friend". The bonhomie is understandable as both countries now face American sanctions and hostility—China for its increasingly apparent role in engineering the Covid-19 pandemic devastating the world and its increasing aggression, and Russia for its revanchism in Europe and cyber-interference in American affairs.

But despite all the nice sounding rhetoric, the reality of the China-Russia relationship is a hollow one. The USA and the nations friendly to it are bound by a set of common values, formal military alliances and/or structures and even sharing of intelligence, with both qualitative and quantitative expansions like the Quad (USA, Japan, India and Australia) happening. There is nothing even remotely comparable in the case of Russia and China; in this partnership, which is purely transactional without any real political integration, Russia is very much the junior partner, with China eyeing its geographically vast, resource-rich but under-populated Eurasian neighbour.

The Uyghurs

Reports about the treatment of the Uyghurs in general and their pregnant women in particular sound barbaric. If the purpose is family planning, fair enough, but it should be implemented by law and not by force. True, Muslims are reputed to procreate much more prolifically than other people, but that does not mean that the Chinese government should resort to violent means to achieve smaller families? Who are the Uyghurs? They are the largest, mostly Muslim ethnic group in China's north-western province of Xinjiang. China has been accused of committing crimes and possibly genocide against the Uyghur population.

According to the Hadith, Prophet Muhammad once asked a man whether he was married. The answer was in the negative. Muhammad reacted by saying: "Then you are a brother of the devil". In Islam, even ascetic orders are expected to marry rather than remain single. One of the Prophet's companions Othman ibn Maz' n wished to lead a life of celibacy; Muhammad forbade him. In the same context, the Prophet exhorted his followers to marry women who would love their husbands and be very prolific, "for I wish you to be more numerous than any other people" (*Mishkat al-Masabih*).

We in India have had a long experience of being ruled by Muslim sultans and, of course, coexisting with them for centuries in all parts of the country. This included prolonged oppression in the 50-year reign of Aurangzeb which ended in 1707. In 1887, the then most prominent Islamic leader Sir Syed Ahmad Khan of Aligarh fame declared in a public speech that the Hindus and Muslims were separate nations. He repeated his contention the following year.

The next eminence to pronounce the same sentiments in early 20th century was Justice Syed Ameer Ali. Then in 1930, the Poet Muhammad Iqbal voiced that Muslims should have a separate homeland even if inside an Indian confederation. Most Hindu leaders, Gandhi downwards, ignored these statements and continued to believe that the Congress party represented all communities. Rightly or wrongly, because the Congress had members of all communities, the leaders presumed that all of their communities followed the party. Eventually, Muhammad Ali Jinnah had the Pakistan Resolution passed by the Muslim League at its Lahore session on 23 March 1940. Yet, the Hindus took only limited notice; nor did the British realise how serious was the Muslim desire for a separate homeland, a New Medina.

On 16 August 1946, the Bengal CM Suhrawardy directed a massive pogrom later known as the Great Calcutta killings, which over three days saw the bloody end of thousands of Hindus. This was Jinnah's way of proving to the British that

Hindus and Muslims could not coexist in the same country. India had to be divided. This is also based on the Islamic theology that Muslims need a *Dar-ul-Islam*, wherein Muslims can flourish and fulfill themselves. Today, India still hosts more Muslims than any country except Indonesia. This is an unusual paradox. If so many Muslims can happily live in India, where was the need of Partition? Yet, the Hindus have accepted this contradiction without a protest. My question is—if the Hindus can be so tolerant, why cannot the Hans of China be considerate enough to let the Uyghurs be?

After all, China has to coexist with many other peoples and countries. There are 57 Islamic countries and they have not yet protested. Why? Possibly because of sheer fear or business interests. But for how long? Sooner or later, the Islamic fury will explode.

In a spirit of freedom and brotherhood, we allowed the Ayodhya litigation to go on for nearly a century, waiting for a court judgment. Only then have we begun to build a temple for Lord Ram whom Poet Iqbal had described as Imam-e-Hind. The Muslims of Ayodhya were in favour of building the temple because it would multiply pilgrimage and consequently bring prosperity. The fight was about an edifice which had no minarets, and no *woozu* for washing hands and feet before proceeding for worship. In fact, it must have been meant as a *mazar* in memory of Babar after he died.

India has had three Muslim Presidents: Zakir Husain, Fakhruddin Ali Ahmed and Abdul Kalam, plus several judges including Supreme Court chief justices and election commissioners appointed by, of course, Hindu governments.

When it comes to elections, all adult citizens have the right to vote. There is no discrimination. In the bargain, the Muslims in the earlier elections voted en masse for one party and it kept winning. The others were slack in casting their votes. This was tolerated and no action was taken to stop this practice. The easy solution was compulsory voting, which would have neutralised en masse voting. But the Hindu ethos was too liberal for a drastic measure although a dozen countries led by Belgium and Australia practice it.

The Chinese Communist Party's Centenary

Whatever be the state of Sino-Indian relations, one does wish the Communist Party of China (CPC) many happy returns of the day as it celebrates a hundred years of its existence. Ironically, the CPC's continuing life is of benefit to India. China's Communist Party owns its country's army which last fought a war in 1979. The CPC has substantial share holdings in a number of large corporations; for example in Alibaba of Jack Ma. Yet, in its centenary celebrations, the Party and its president-for-life, who may be more appropriately called Emperor Xi Jinping, betray an inadmissible nervousness. In the very opening session of the CPC's centenary celebrations, Xi Jinping has warned that "Foreign powers will have their heads bashed if they try to bully China"—hardly a confident opening note for a nation that dreams of being numero uno in the world. What makes China or the CPC nervous?

With development and prosperity, the class profile of the people will change. Rich and aware citizens will want to have their say. A mere political dictatorship will not be tolerated forever; the party has to share power with the people. Therefore, the CPC has itself become a large investor. No one is a bigger businessperson in China than the CPC. If there be any rebellion, the Chinese army or the People's Liberation Army (PLA) cannot be a part of it because it is employed by the Party.

China had learnt a lesson in 1989 in the Tiananmen Square episode when the Army had mowed down thousands of young men and women. Singapore's then prime minister who had watched the events on television later wrote that "it was unbelievable". The PLA had turned its guns on its own people. Tanks and armoured personnel carriers stormed into the streets leading to the Square to fire upon protestors. All that the agitators wanted was to register their protest against corruption, nepotism and inflation. They wanted the CPC and the regime to reform.

Writing in his autobiography, Lee Kwan Yew, the man who made Singapore what it is today, pointed out four great challenges in China's future. People would demand more active participation in the affairs of the state. The Tiananmen episode has already given an early warning. There are likely to be more tensions as income differences widen, not only between the people but between the prosperous coastal and riverine provinces and the poorer inland provinces, as well as between the Han heartland and Mongolia, Tibetan and the Uyghur people.

As the economy is further modernised, there may well be a breakdown in the banking system and large-scale unemployment following reforms of state enterprises—if the CPC ever allows it. Corruption is a pernicious disease, although it may not seem obvious today. The biggest challenge for China will be to adjust to the shift from a controlled or planned economy to a market one; also from a communist society to a free civil society. The Chinese rulers have been aware that this evolution could cause serious dislocations and even end the CPC's rule, possibly setting off disintegrative forces. Therefore, the party has to own the army.

An international challenge will be adjustments in interacting with the other countries, which have different ethical values and moral standards. The Chinese people have never been very religious. As a wag told us in Hong Kong, "We are not like you Indians. We are Buddhists at breakfast, Confucians at lunch and Taoists at dinner. We are very different from you Hindus and Muslims," he stressed. This difference is probably the reason why the Chinese appear to be deceptive from the smallest questions to the biggest issues. They do not really realise that they have surprised and upset the others. The loud signs that they have antagonised most nations of the world are noticeable today. The Chinese probably expect to push through with their economic muscle, but economic glitter does not stand on its own.

Morality and ethics are sophisticated expressions but without the fear of punishment, they are likely to be hollow—be it the fear of society, of law or of God; or for example the Hindu fear that one's *dushkarma* (bad deeds) will result in *durbhagya* (ill fate). To an extent, Indian Muslims and Christians, at least some of them, also believe in karma. This is perhaps a throwback to the period when their forefathers were Hindus. But when none of these factors operate, most individuals are likely to indulge in selfish actions without any inhibitions. Scholars of ethics do sometimes mention conscience as an important factor. That may be, but for a comparatively few persons. The Hindu faith depends so much on karma that in Hindi and many Indian languages there is no precise word for conscience. There is one in Urdu—namely, *zameer*. I wonder if there is any equivalent in the Chinese language.

In short, the Chinese obey the law when they must, and that is all. Other than that, the question of right and wrong, the issue of moral and immoral does not arise for an average Chinese. When a Chinese, whether individually or collectively, resorts to anything unethical, it is because he is ignorant about morality. He may not be aware that he has done something wrong. The Chinese are equally ignorant about their food; what they should eat and should not. Over the ages, they have eaten every bird and animal available in their country. During my 14-day visit to China, I was able to see some colourful birds at what used to be the Guangzhou Zoo. Thereafter, I saw them in open carts driven by two ponies. Once, on a highway going southwards from Shanghai, our car was overtaken by a lorry full of pigs. Those were the live birds and animals I saw; the rest were dead snakes floating in water contained in large glass jars. We were told by the waiter that consumption of such water makes one stronger. These sights were common in large and posh restaurants.

While Hindus treat some of the fauna as the vehicles of deities, such as the mouse being the mount of Ganesha and the swan of Goddess Saraswati and so on, the Chinese treat them as part of their diet. To sum it up, the people of the Yellow Kingdom put a great deal of stress in the efficacy of force and violence. In his concluding advice to party workers the late Mao Zedong asserted that "Political power grows out of the barrel of a gun".

China: A Stitch in Time

It is true that Xi Jinping's China is by now sufficiently worked up for whatever reasons. It also is increasingly apparent that China has to be stopped in its tracks if the world is not to plunge into a devastating war. Had Europe, Britain and France in particular, done likewise in 1936, WWII would have probably been averted. Notwithstanding Germany being bound by the Treaty of Versailles in 1919, and forced to downsize its military, its Fuhrer Adolf Hitler ordered his troops to seize the demilitarised Rhineland—formerly German territory—in 1936, in complete violation of the Treaty. No European power did or even said anything. Germany's generals, who were then reluctant to precipitate another armed conflict, began having faith in their Fuhrer's supposed strategic calibre.

In 1938, just two years after Rhineland, Britain's Prime Minister Neville Chamberlain and France's PM Edouard Daladier promptly accepted Hitler's invitation to a conference in Munich to settle the Sudetenland issue. This Czechoslovakian province was substantially German-speaking. The Fuhrer wanted it for the greater glory of his fatherland. The visiting leaders promptly conceded this demand without so much as even consulting the Czechoslovaks. Chamberlain publicly eulogised the success of this conference as having achieved "peace in our time". This conclusively convinced the Germans that their Fuhrer knew what he was doing.

The inevitable happened thereafter. Austria was the next to be gobbled up as part of greater Germany, without a shot being fired. In September the following year, Poland was overrun in less than six weeks, with France capitulating in a similar fashion in 1940. Had the French and British resisted Nazi Germany, which was militarily less prepared in 1936, Hitler would possibly have lost power or stayed away from such military adventures.

China is much better prepared economically and militarily. It has progressed by leaps and bounds, particularly after Deng Xiaoping. But how far would it have gone had the American gates for its goods not opened up? China's goods are not products of its own technology, but the result of very diligent copying, politely called 'reverse engineering'. The cheap cost of Chinese goods can be attributed to virtually free grants of land and throwaway interest rates for term loans to local entrepreneurs and, of course, low wages to its workers, at least in the early phase of China's meteoric rise.

This is in contrast to Japan's products—automobiles, electronic goods, computers, watches, et al. These are not only original but also largely unsurpassed by other countries. Militarily too, unlike Japan, China does not have a sufficient tradition. Strangely, the People's Liberation Army (PLA), China's armed force, belongs to the Communist Party of China and *not* to the country. Moreover, China's armed forces are not made up of volunteers but mostly conscripts. It is one thing for anyone to be prepared to give his life for his country; it is difficult to fight with the same spirit for a political party which can rise and fall. There can be factional feuds too within a party, which partly explains a vast number of Chinese soldiers losing their lives in skirmishes and small battles they have been involved in, over the last few decades. Also, more crucially, the Chinese armed forces have not been involved in fighting since 1979 when they invaded Vietnam, a war where they took a beating.

Battle-experience is more important than training in order to be a good soldier. A battle-hardened soldier is far more dependable than a well-trained recruit. Anyone who has not faced bullets is unpredictable in a combat situation, as to how he would react when the shooting begins. Today's PLA may not have a single soldier who has faced actual combat.

In the meantime, the aggressive behaviour displayed by China's political leadership has antagonised many countries. North Korea and Pakistan apart, it is difficult to think of a Chinese ally. While North Korea's army is large and marches excellently in military parades, it has not faced a bullet since 1953. In contrast, the Indian army was originally founded by the British, who were amongst the best trained armed forces other than the German ones. India has fought five wars, as well as continual insurgencies in eastern India and Kashmir.

China is presumably militarily mighty. Taiwan is a major issue with the current leadership in Beijing. The South China Sea is another flashpoint. The Himalayas in India's north are potentially the third one. There are Japan and Taiwan, which for their size have excellent air forces. There is Australia further south. All that is necessary is for the USA to open its treasury of advanced weaponry. The rest of the allies are strong enough to halt the yellow giant from going any farther, if not actually force it to take a few steps back in its aggressiveness.

This is also imperative because China's much-hyped rise has actually happened. In other words, China is no longer rising but has risen. The window of opportunity to grab global hegemony is closing and that makes the situation very dangerous.

The Olympic Games

A great deal of effort and money was invested in the 1982 Asian Games. However, at a swimming event, the guest-in-chief was one of our cine superstars. When he approached the podium to award the medals, the audience erupted in wild applause, as if the winners did not matter; the gold, silver and bronze winners of that event were not Indian. The coach of one of the winning teams asked who this chief guest was, to which the rather chirpy reply was: "Don't you know him? He is our most famous cine superstar". To this, the coach's pithy response was: "I now understand why such a vast country like India is nowhere in sport".

Except for a few privileged families, sports were not considered an integral part of life in Indian society. If one goes back to the times of Mahabharata, archery and *gada* (iron mace) contests were a part of the education of the Pandava and Kaurava princes with Dronacharya being the main teacher. In the war that followed between the Kauravas and the Pandavas, their guru Dronacharya was an army commander. Sports did not travel or touch villages until recently. The state governments seldom took any interest and most of the sports associations were treated by their members as small political arenas for their self-promotion. As a result, regional representation was more important than the potential of the player.

The Duke of Wellington once remarked: "The battle of Waterloo was won on the playing fields of Eton". He evidently implied how sports helped to make young men into capable military officers. Sports help to build the physique, introduce strategy and tactics in the lives of young men (and women) and teach them how to outwit the opponent. It is true that the East India Company and later the British Government employed a fair number of Indian soldiers, but as a rule, they confined their choice to what they felt were the 'martial' communities. These did not add up to very many persons in such a vast country. In any case, most of those selected were employed as sepoys.

Over the centuries, most Indians kept themselves away from sport except for cricket in which modern facilities have been available in the cities. Even these were not affordable by the poor although the Board of Control for Cricket in India (BCCI) is rolling in wealth.

Perhaps we should pay sufficient attention to setting up an academy for the poor, which provides for the vital need of diet and nourishment which may be unaffordable for many a family in our country. In this context, the state government of Odisha deserves praise for patronising hockey as a sport. On the contrary, West Bengal which was doing well in football allowed its clubs to bring players from others states and even from overseas. In the process, its own players declined in numbers as well as quality. If other states could choose other games like Odisha, it would be a great national service. Here, it is important to note that we were monopolists of the Olympic gold medal in hockey until 1960. Today, we celebrate our men's hockey team winning a bronze medal in the Tokyo Olympics 2020. Apart from the decline, hockey was an illustration of how not to be smug about one's success. As an instance, Indian players kept dribbling the ball very skillfully while the rest of the world had adopted the technique of passing the ball from player to player. For several players, Indian hockey could not adjust to the advent of astro turf or mandatory wearing of shoes. Earlier, there were years when our hockey wizards won because they played barefoot.

In the 1936 Berlin Olympics, India faced Germany in the hockey final. At half-time, India led Germany by only 1-0. Maharaja Sayajirao Gaekwad of Baroda was concerned and went down to the dressing room. He advised Dhyan Chand to play barefoot for the remainder of the match. The eventual score was India-5, Germany-1; Dhyan Chand had scored a hat-trick. The result was not pleasing to Führer Adolf Hitler, who was also a part of the audience. Nevertheless, he called Dhyan Chand later and offered him the rank of a colonel if the latter were to come over to Germany as its citizen.

Incidentally, the Olympic Games were started some 3,500 years in Greece as a mark of homage to God Zeus. To begin with there were many Greek city states which gathered at the city of Olympia. In the early games, the events were very few, but soon they increased and chariot racing and even horse racing came in. There were no medals but wreaths and garlands. When the Romans conquered the Greek cities, the

Games carried on until Emperor Theodosius I in 393 AD, who particularly disapproved of the young men (there were no women participants) stripping. The Games were revived at the initiative of Baron Coubertin of France in 1896 at Athens.

The numbers of countries as well as the players have been progressively increasing, except at Moscow in 1980, when the Soviet Union had invaded Afghanistan and 60 eligible nations, mostly western, boycotted the Games. The 1972 Munich Games were marred by terrorists who killed a dozen Israeli participants.

Olympiads Recalled

The Olympic Games were named after the Greek city state Olympia, where the event began in 776 BC. They were ended in 393 AD by Roman Emperor Theodosius, who strongly disapproved of participants having to completely strip; stitching of cloth had not been introduced until then in Europe to make underwear.

The architect of the modern games was one Baron Pierre de Coubertin. Athens in Greece was chosen as the first host as a tribute to ancient Olympia. Until 1912, apart from the gold, silver and bronze medals, the next five participants were awarded diplomas. In the first games women competed at golf, lawn tennis and archery.

Due to WWI, the next Olympiad was held in Belgium in 1920. Until 1936 was the golden age of athletics with Finland dominating the middle and long-distance running. Jesse Owens became a legend; so did Dhyan Chand as a hockey genius in 1928 and 1936.

Berlin 1936 was the 10th occurrence of the modern Olympic Games. The 1936 Olympics were held in a tense, politically charged atmosphere. The Nazi Party had risen to power in 1933, two years after Berlin was awarded the Games, and its racist policies led to international debate about a boycott of the Games. Fearing a mass boycott, the International Olympic Committee pressured the German government and received assurances that qualified Jewish athletes would be part of the German team and that the Games would not be used to promote Nazi ideology.

But Adolf Hitler's government wasn't serious about delivering on those promises. Only one athlete of Jewish descent, Helene Mayer, was a member of the German team; pamphlets and speeches about the "natural superiority" of the Aryan race were commonplace. The Reich Sports Field, a newly-constructed sports complex was draped in Nazi banners and symbols. Nonetheless, the attraction of the Olympiad prevailed and 49 countries chose to attend the Berlin Olympic Games.

The 1936 Berlin Olympics are also famed for an Indo-German encounter. Our hockey legend Dhyan Chand won the admiration of Germany's Fuhrer. The Germans had defeated the Indian team 4-1 in a practice match, sending a warning to a complacent Indian squad basking in the old glory of two previous gold medals in 1928 and 1932. Germany and India reached the finals. In the grandstand sat Hitler, confident of Germany winning the match on the strength of the practice match results.

The Germans had already sent an invitation to the Indian team for a social evening to fete the victors. In the first half, the Indians were unable to pierce the German defence. In one rally by Dhyan Chand, the German goalkeeper collided with him and the goalkeeper's hockey stick struck him in the face. Dhyan Chand collapsed on the field and had to be carried out. He then changed from stud-soled shoes to playing barefoot upon the advice of the Maharaja of Baroda, also a visitor to the Games. The game resumed with the Germans playing aggressively. But India's captain played a mesmerising game, controlling the ball as if by divine wizardry and fired in three quick goals. The final score was India 5, Germany 1.

At the evening function, a German officer came to Dhyan Chand and said the Fuhrer wanted to meet him. Dhyan Chand himself recalled the encounter 20 years later: "I did a *salaam* to the Fuhrer. Hitler scanned me from top to bottom".

"You are the hockey wizard everyone is blaming for turning the tables in today's match. I am told you had an injury in the match. How are you now?" the Fuhrer asked. The translator translated from German to English. Dhyan Chand smiled and looked calmly at Hitler and replied that he had "left a tooth in Germany in the match but was otherwise fine". He also thanked Hitler for his fine hospitality.

Hitler smiled when he heard the answer and asked Dhyan Chand about his occupation, to which the latter replied he was a corporal in the Indian army. The Fuhrer recalled that he too had been a corporal in his young days. Impressed by Dhyan Chand's ability and prowess, he asked him to join the German army as an officer. Following a stunned silence, Dhyan Chand thanked Hitler for his generous offer but told him that India was his home. Hitler nodded his head slightly, looked at him again and moved on.

Although not happy at Germany's defeat to India in the finals, this result did not cause any heartburn among the Nazis, as Indians were regarded as Indo-Aryans and, therefore, 'acceptable'. What really turned Hitler's bile was American star Jesse Owen's sweep of four athletic medals, something Hitler could not stomach.

Since the revival of the Games, growth in the number of competitions, of competitors, and of participating countries has been almost continuous. It took some time for the Games to find a pattern of continuity. Athens in 1896, Paris in 1900, and St Louis, Missouri in 1904 were somewhat haphazard affairs. At Stockholm in 1912, the number of nations increased to 28. For the first time, three swimming events for women were included. No games were held in 1916 because of World War I.

This period saw the golden age of athletes—from the Finnish domination of middle and long-distance running to the performances in the sprints, especially that of Jesse Owens. In less than two years after the Armistice in November 1918, Belgium organised the first post-World War I Olympics at Antwerp. Twenty-nine nations, including many new ones, sent more than 2,500 competitors to take part in them. Women competitors were still a mere handful (about 60). Four years later, in Paris, the number of countries increased to 44 with more than 3,000 competitors.

In 1928 in Amsterdam, women's track and field competitions (five events) and one event for women in gymnastics were introduced. Four years later, the Games for the second time crossed the Atlantic to Los Angeles but the number of competitors fell to less than 1,500 from 37 countries.

The long journey from Europe and the Great Depression were responsible for the decrease. The return to Europe for the Berlin Games produced 4,000 athletes in 1936.

No Games were held in 1940 or 1944 because of World War II. London was given the task of organising the first post-war Games in 1948 with a bare three years available. This was accomplished despite difficult post-war conditions. Fifty-nine countries with 4,000 competitors participated.

Finland hosted the 1952 Games at Helsinki, and in 1956, for the first time the venue was in the Southern Hemisphere at Melbourne in Australia. Equestrian events had to take place in another country because of quarantine regulations that prohibited the importation of horses to Australia; they were held in Stockholm. Again the distance from Europe reduced the competitors in Melbourne by 1,500. After Rome in 1960, the Olympics were held in Asia for the first time in 1964, at Tokyo, in a city where the previous award (in 1940) had not been fulfilled.

The Olympics have also been marked by political violence and dissension. In the Munich Olympics in 1972, tragedy struck the Games when Arab (Palestinian) terrorists invaded the Olympic Village and killed nine Israeli athletes taken as hostages for the release of 200 Arab prisoners in Israel. At the Montreal Olympics in 1976, the Canadian government refused visas to the representatives of Taiwan because they were unwilling to forgo the title of the Republic of China, under which their National Olympic Committee was admitted to the IOC.

The 1980 Moscow Olympics were marred by the boycott of 60 nations in protest against the Soviet Union's invasion of Afghanistan in December 1979. The Moscow Games were further diminished by the intrusion of two other issues—alleged bias in judging by East European officials and the use of anabolic steroids by athletes to improve performance. The 1984 Los Angeles Olympics suffered a boycott by the Soviet Union and a number of its allies as retaliation for the Western boycott of the 1980 Moscow Olympics.

Veto or Sayonara UNO

Prime Minister Narendra Modi had not too long ago presided over the UN Security Council meeting called by India. However, the UNO has been a non-achiever so far. For example, in 1999, the then UN Secretary General Kofi Annan suddenly flew into Delhi to 'mediate' in the ongoing Kargil War, only to be politely told by the Vajpayee government to mind his own business and go back. It is reported that this international body has some 100,000 employees from the senior-most to the junior-most. If the average cost of these men and women is taken to be $50,000 per head, it means an expenditure of five thousand million or five billion dollars annually. The organisation's other expenses are separate.

The late American columnist Charles Krauthammer had dubbed the UN a "corrupt impostor, undeserving of any American support". Some others have even more pejoratively called it the 'Useless Non-existent Organisation'. Titled 'A Table for Tyrants', former Czech President Vaclav Havel wrote an article in *The New York Times* in May 2009, saying that he felt scandalised when he saw the UN Human Rights Council filled with members like Sudan, Zimbabwe, China and Saudi Arabia, which have no human rights.

Yet, India continues to be an elephantine contributor to the UN peacekeeping contingents, and has sent nearly 200,000 peacekeepers to 44 missions over the years. This is more than the national armed forces of most countries. Indian forces working for the UN have suffered more casualties than any other country's armed forces. Indian policymakers argue that this is being done not for any strategic gain but in the service of 'global ideals' like strengthening the world body, and international peace and security. The UN did not even condemn communist China's unprovoked aggression against a democratic India in October 1962, leave alone do anything about it. The irony is that the dictatorial, communist China enjoys a permanent seat in the Security Council while India, the world's largest democracy, does not.

The only service the UN arguably performed was to provide a platform for radical communist elements and a whole generation of dictators and autocrats to portray themselves as leaders and statesman. Most notable in this regard was India's Krishna Menon, whose vitriolic anti-Western rhetoric and fire-spitting speeches in the UN earned him the dubious sobriquet of a "spitting camel". He was so dubbed by the Americans who hated Menon's patronising lecturing, but also more seriously earned India a lot of Western ill-will.

The failures of the UNO make an unusually long catalogue beginning with 1948. That year, the Soviet Union blockaded Berlin. The only action that prevented the city's surrender was the American airlift of all conceivable supplies in the spirit of *Ich bin ein Berliner* (I am a Berliner), the famous speech of President Kennedy on 26 June 1963 in West Berlin.

In the Korean War (1950-53), the communist North had gone all out to take over the entire peninsula. Again, the UNO could do nothing. It watched Vietnam being bombed more intensively than anywhere, anytime, since or before WWII. The UNO, however, remained silent and inactive as ever. In 1956, the Anglo-French invasion allied with Israel against Egypt over the Suez Canal issue; this yet again proved UN incompetence. It failed again the same year when the Soviet Union invaded Hungary. In 1959, the world witnessed the abduction and rape of Tibet by China. In 1968, the international body looked askance at the Prague Spring when Soviet tanks rolled into Czechoslovakia. The catalogue of UN acts of omission continues to be legendary.

As historians William H Harbaugh and Ronald E Powaski point out, Theodore Roosevelt was the first American President to call for an international league. At the acceptance of his Nobel Prize, Roosevelt said: "It would be a masterstroke if those great powers honestly bent on peace would form a League of Peace". Such an idea should logically have emerged from Europe, whose long history is a record of almost unending wars. At the end of the Great War the League of Nations came up in the hope of ending the era of war, and giving the West an age of peace. Yet again, this idea emerged from an American President Woodrow Wilson.

But the credibility of the League of Nations was weakened by the fact that the United States never joined the League; and the Soviet Union joined late but was soon expelled after invading Finland. Germany withdrew from the League, as did Japan, Italy, Spain and others. The onset of the Second World War showed that the League had failed its primary purpose, which was to prevent any future world war. The League lasted for 26 years. The United Nations (UN) replaced it after the end of the Second World War and inherited several agencies and organisations spawned by the League.

True, the League of Nations did not last long. Yet, credit must go to the League for having founded the International Court of Justice and the International Labour Organisation and other bodies. It is doubtful the UN would leave behind anything memorable except its performance of profligacy. It is high time India told the Security Council to give it a Permanent Seat with veto power. If the Council gives it, well and good, or else, New Delhi should resign from the organisation and thus save itself time, money and honour.

Who are The Taliban?

The Taliban in neighbouring Afghanistan are very much in the news after the sudden collapse of the Afghan regime of Ashraf Ghani and the swift takeover of that country by the Talib hordes. But who are the Taliban? To learn about them, we must turn our attention to Deoband, barely 300 kms away from our capital Delhi.

The Deoband *madrasa* was set up in 1867 as a reaction against the end of what remained of the Mughal Empire following the defeat of the Sepoy Mutiny of 1857-58. The seminary's objective was to preserve Islamic learning and way of life. It began with one teacher Mulla Mahmud Deobandi and was originally known as the Arab madrasa. There were those who swore vengeance on the British. Out of these movements emerged the Taliban, though much later, as well as Al Qaeda, with global aspirations.

In the period Pakistan's military dictator General Zia-ul-Haq was fervently Islamising Pakistan, the Taliban first emerged in Afghanistan as a cohesive unit. Rahimullah Yusufzai, a Peshawar-based scholarly journalist in an interface with Charles Allen, a renowned historian of the British Raj (and grandson of the founder of *The Pioneer* daily) reported being the first journalist to note the appearance of the Taliban on the Afghan scene in 1994. They were unsmiling youngsters with untrimmed beards, black turbans, black waistcoats, carrying either Kalashnikov automatic rifles or grenade launchers.

In 1879, the Deoband madrasa assumed the additional name of Dar-ul-Uloom, or the abode of Islamic learning.
English was prohibited; and all students had to learn the Quran and the Hadith in Arabic. This was in accordance with the teachings of Shah Waliullah of Delhi. The madrasa retained militant jihad as a central pillar of the faith. Officially, Deoband has rejected *ijtihad* ((the use of independent reasoning) in matters of the Sharia. Around the end of the 19th century, the teachings at the madrasa were traditional and termed Salafi, or following the forefathers based on the ideas of renowned jurists Hanabali and Ibn Taymiyyah. The ideology preached at the institution has worldwide influence. A true Muslim's first duty is to defend his religion wherever it is under attack. Sunni Islam of South Asia has been impacted the most by these teachings.

The Jamiat Ulema-e-Hind (JUH), the Party of Clerics of Hindustan formed in 1920 later resulted in two splinter groups: Tablighi Jamiat (Preaching Party) led by Naqshbandi Sufi Maulana Muhammad Ilyas followed the teachings of Shah Waliullah. The second was led by Mawdudi, who promoted a new political agenda. For him, Islam had to present itself as a viable political and social alternative to both Western capitalism and socialism. He advocated a new political platform based on Islamic revival and separation through political action and jihad. Islam had to confront non-Islam head on. Out of the Islamic revolution would emerge the Islamic state purged of all accretions, that is a 'democratic' caliphate whose citizens would embrace Sharia willingly. In 1939, Mawdudi moved to Lahore. Two years later, he founded Jamiat-e-Islami (JI) in direct opposition to JUH. As the demand for a separate Muslim state grew in India, a number of Deobandis formed another outfit, the Jamiat-e-Ulema-e-Islam or party of scholars of Islam in 1945, under the leadership of Maulana Shabbar Ahmad Othmani and Maulana Mufti Mahmud. The aim of the party was to shape the upcoming nation of Pakistan into a truly Muslim state with an Islamic Constitution in conformity with the Quran and Sharia, a vision it shared with the Tablighi Jamaat.

By 1941, on the eve of Partition, there were around two hundred madrasas in Pakistan, rising to 893 by 1972. Of these, 354 were Deobandi; 144 Al-Hadith and 267 Barelvis. By 1980, nearly 70 percent of the madrasas were controlled by Deobandis. By 2002, their number was 10,000; of these 7,000 belonged to Deobandis. Going by this trend, all madrasas would now be under the control of Deobandis. Such is the extent of influence of the institution based in Deoband.

Most of the Taliban are the products of these madrasas, which have become nurseries for producing the Taliban. The various fundamentalist organisations that exist now in India and Pakistan are one way or the other connected to the Deoband madrasa. The Taliban in Pakistan and Afghanistan have acknowledged the inspiration received from Deoband (India).

Charles Allen in his book *God's Terrorists* points out that Wahhabism is the guiding ideology behind modern Islamist terrorism. The Taliban are representatives of this ideology in action. Allen mentions that Ahmad Rashid has meticulously captured the rise of Taliban in his book, *Taliban: The Story of the Warlords*. In Rashid's words: 'The Taliban represent nobody but themselves and recognise no Islam but their own'.

The Shia Revival says that the Deobandi area of influence stretches from Bangladesh to southern Afghanistan. The Deobandis became associated with the Afghan War in 1980s. Many other South Asia's Sunni extremists responsible for violence hail from the Deobandi tradition. The Pakistani-trained Taliban committed violence against the Afghan Hazaras. They declared Afghan Shias to be infidels and massacred at least two thousand of them in Mazar-e-Sharif and Bamiyan in 1997-98. Others have been told to convert to Sunnism or face death.

Sri Lanka's Food Emergency

Since 1964, I have been in touch with Sri Lanka intermittently. At that time, I was told that the butter and the ice cream they ate came from New Zealand. Many of the vegetables were also imported, including from India. On 31 August 2021, Sri Lanka declared a national 'food emergency'. The country ran out of foreign exchange, and its government overspent on development by borrowing from China, a greedy lender. The takeover of the country's Hambantota port by the lender was a signal that what Sri Lanka could not pay back China in cash, it was having to fork out in kind, namely real estate at the cost of its sovereignty.

Two characteristics of the Sinhalese people I have noted are: one, they love life and enjoy themselves when the going is good. Two, they are a little suspicious of Indians, because of the Tamils. They fear that someday a situation may arise whereby India may have to take over Sri Lanka. Given identical lending terms by India and China, they would prefer the latter. The presumption is that the Beijing is far away whereas Delhi is next door, along with its Tamils. The food emergency having to be declared is the result of the focus on 'today'; tomorrow and the day after will take care of themselves.

Right after its independence, Sri Lanka (then Ceylon) did not focus on growing its staple food on a sufficient scale. In the early days and for years, the country concentrated on tending its tea gardens, rubber and copra trees. The foreign exchange earnings were so plentiful that there used to be a picnic of imported goods. The first painful pinch was felt in 1964. NM Perera was the finance minister and he went to Parliament to pass very stringent laws. After working for a lifetime, on retirement foreigners were allowed to remit only Rs 75,000 (for Indians) and Rs 2,50,000 (for others). The discrimination was severe. Had the Indian High Commissioner not been very helpful, my father-in-law could not have got permission to remit a total of Rs 1,50,000 after working in a British Company for 32 years, all in Sri Lanka. Such was the foreign exchange famine suddenly discovered.

I must confess, though, that the management at New Delhi was no better. In 1990, the Indian treasury had run out of foreign exchange. In order not to fail its commitments overseas, the government sent many crates of gold to banks in London. Fortunately, in 1991, India was gifted with a decisive Prime Minister PV Narasimha Rao who liberalised and globalised the Indian economy. He thus brought about an economic revolution.

A small country is vulnerable both economically as well as politically. Its government must play its part very cautiously. Sri Lanka liberalised before India and recovered from the cave-in of 1964 that is described above. But any significant decline in foreign exchange earnings should be taken seriously. Otherwise, trouble can hit the economy before giving the government a chance to draw in the reins. The picture of the tea industry has been rather sad everywhere, be it Sri Lanka or southern India. But to Sri Lanka, it made a big difference. The price of a plain to medium tea was two rupees per kilogram (although earlier the weight was in pounds) in 1939. By now it should have been (in step with the inflation), 600 to 800 rupees but it is only the equivalent of 200 Indian rupees.

Garments are another Sri Lankan activity. When there is prosperity, it can earn good foreign exchange. On the other hand, when there is a crisis like the current one caused by Covid, there can be a slump in demand. People short of money can do without buying clothes for a year or more. These are the kind of things that brought trouble for Sri Lanka. More so, because the country has borrowings to return. Tourism is another cause of the crisis. It was the largest single foreign exchange earner for Sri Lanka. Due to Covid, tourism has fallen drastically.

In the interim, Sri Lanka virtually ignored India, probably embarrassed by its affair with China. After China claimed the port of Hambantota, things have changed somewhat. The current Indo-Sri Lanka ties have improved. India may offer food grains, wheat, rice and whatever else is available and may also consider swap loans, whose return would be in Sri Lankan rupees. India can buy only Sri Lankan goods with the returned money against the swap loan.

Sri Lanka has been described traditionally as the Emerald Isle. It is indeed a beautiful country with the sea on its periphery. People, especially from the West find it irresistibly attractive.

The beaches are beautiful and monuments of Buddhism are also splendid, whether Anirudhapura, Pollonaruwa or Sigiriya. The Emerald Isle also has a charisma which few other beautiful places have. Its infrastructure for the keen tourist is praiseworthy with its many five star hotels, its transportation et al.

The Unfolding
Afghanistan Story

On 10 November 2021, a regional security dialogue on Afghanisthan was held in New Delhi. India's National Security Advisor (NSA) Ajit Doval was the host. The meeting was attended by NSA's counterparts from five central Asian countries, along with Russia and China.

Such a meeting was unprecedented and indicated how seriously these powers had reacted to the Afghan crisis. To add to it all, China announced an aid package of $31 million to the new regime in Kabul, thus declaring whose side it was on, whether of terrorists or otherwise.

One wonders how an associate of terrorist states and a member of the United Nations, that too a permanent member of its Security Council, is being allowed to get away with such behaviour. On the one hand, the USA and UK publicly condemn terrorism and on the other sit with China on the same Security Council. By doing so, are they not legitimising terrorism? Was the recent Delhi mega meet arranged in order to persuade India to join the coalition to keep the Chinese out of Afghanistan? If at all New Delhi happens to be thinking along these lines, it must recall that Britain failed three times in the 19th century to defeat Afghanistan. Russia, then the Soviet Union, fought for nine years to dominate Afghanistan through proxies backed by its own soldiers. Russia's Afghan adventure was an undiluted failure.

Thereafter, the USA took its turn not once but twice. Both times, it has had to retreat with its tail between its legs. Incidentally, going back further into history, Mughal Emperors Shah Jahan and Aurangzeb had bitter experiences in Afghanistan. Prior to them, Akbar the Great did manage to subdue Afghanistan. The lesson learnt from this history is to think, and think again before committing Indian soldiers to Afghanistan. It is true that Afghanistan owes a great deal to India; the debt began with Mahmud of Ghazni, Shahabuddin Ghori and subsequently Ahmed Shah Abdali.

If people desire to flee Afghanistan, Pakistan would be the first country they would turn to. The next would perhaps be India, either through the Kashmir Valley or the deserts of Rajasthan through the Jaisalmer area; it still remains unfenced. The thrust of this submission is that New Delhi must make sure that Pakistan does not become the Bangladesh of yesterday, teeming with infiltrators.

America's latest concern would be Afghanistan's enormous mineral wealth, which still lies untapped. Washington would hate to see it simply fall into the lap of China. For its part, Russia too would not like China to grow more dominant. Any Chinese ascendancy in Afghanistan would mean a bigger shadow of the dragon on Central Asia, whose borders touch

Russia's Siberia, a vast territory China is eyeing.

An elephant in the room is Erdogan's Turkey, which has spontaneously got interested in Afghanistan. Erdogan has no money to spend, but makes up for it by the enormity of his ambition. The seat of the Caliph of Islam has been considered vacant since Mustafa Kemal Pasha, the Ataturk, abolished the Caliphate in 1924, and exiled its last incumbent. Occupying this seat would make Erdogan the leader of all Sunni Muslims in the world; spiritual as well as temporal. He has not hesitated to jostle with the king of Saudi Arabia to demonstrate that he is more Islamic than the Arabs.

Another reason for Erdogan to get involved in Afghanistan and to flirt with Pakistan is to possibly obtain a few of the latter's nuclear weapons, so that if the need arises, he could blackmail either Russia or Europe, or both. Erdogan has been harbouring Ottomanesque ambitions for quite long. Under him, Turkey has all but abandoned its quest to become a European country. Its long-practiced secularism, too, now seems in danger of being washed away in the rising tide of neo-Islamism. Such a neo-Ottomanesque Turkey acquiring nuclear weapons will undoubtedly be a nightmare for Europe and the whole world. The silent equations being pursued with Delhi could be a pointer.

Hitherto, there was no great relationship between Turkey and Afghanistan. Erdogan and his predecessors had positioned Turkey in such a manner that it was a part of Europe. In fact, Kemal Ataturk had consistently felt that the future of Turkey lay in Europe. He asked his people to dress like Europeans and follow the European way of life. He converted the alphabet of the Turkish language from the Arabic script to Roman in three months, and also had the Quran written in Turkish. Ataturk was undoubtedly a visionary.

This visionary plan has been disturbed due to the outbreak of a war between Islamic jihad and five continents. In other words, Islamic terrorism has made Turkey unwelcome in Europe and, hence, its new endeavour to spread its tentacles in Central and South Asia.

The Stasi Report on Secularism

Without there being a consensus or a clarification on what comprises secularism, the Manmohan Singh-led coalition ministry was meant to be bound together on its basis. Eulogies to secularism appear frequently enough in the media, but seldom is a mention made of the Bernard Stasi report, which was a thesis on what is a secular state. It was submitted on 11 December 2003 and was treated as the backgrounder for the secular law which was passed by the French National Assembly on 15 March 2004. The difficulty is that the report is not readily available in an English translation. The 76-page thesis describes and defines secularism. The three essential principles are: freedom of conscience, equality in law for spiritual and religious beliefs, and neutrality of political power.

The law framed in March that year attempted to implement these principles; it did not abolish the wearing of either Jewish skull caps or Muslim headscarves. All that it ordained was that the students attending government schools or employees working in government offices must not display religious symbols of a conspicuous nature which would include even a large cross. There was no restriction on wearing of any form of dress or display of any religious symbols in the country at large. The state, however, had to maintain absolute neutrality between one religion and another. The French insistence on secularism or the absolute separation of the Church from the State goes back to 1905, when in December that year, a Republican Law was passed by the National Assembly. Its Article 1 assured the liberty of conscience. It guaranteed the free exercise of religious beliefs; the only restrictions were decreed in the interest of public order.

Article 2 states that the Republic does not recognise either salaries paid or subsidies granted to any religious group. The Stasi Report has stated that Islam is believed to be incompatible with secularism. This was the conclusion to the investigation carried out by Bernard Stasi and the subsequent passing of the legislation. As far as private employers of schools are concerned, the law is that the will of the institution would prevail and not any idiosyncrasy of the employee. The intention behind the stipulation is to ensure that there is no discrimination against members of any religion, so that an employer does not avoid the appointment of a scarf-wearing lady or a skull cap-wearing man.

These provisions ensure not only the neutrality of political authority but also the freedom of conscience and belief, as well as equality before the law. The Stasi Report emphasised secularism as a cornerstone of a democracy.

Every state is sovereign and has the right to frame its Constitution as well as its other laws according to the needs of its society. How else has Malaysia declared itself an Islamic

Republic completely overlooking the presence of Hindus, Buddhists and Christians who comprise nearly half of the population? Why should Bangladesh and Pakistan have the privilege to call themselves Islamic? Bangladesh had reduced its Hindu population to 10 percent by 1991. In 1947, Hindus comprised 30 percent of East Bengal. Pakistan has today, according to its own census figures, only 1.5 percent Hindus. The rest have suffered ethnic cleansing. The fact that India has never challenged the rights of Bangladesh or Pakistan to do what they have done means that we have respected their sovereignty.

Going further, would the Emirates in Asia be justified in not allowing a temple to be built on their territory? Should Saudi Arabia have the right to disallow even the entry of a non-Muslim on the soil of Mecca and Medina? Does any universal declaration of human rights apply to these respected members of the international community in general, and the UNO in particular? The Stasi Report has clarified that Article 9 of the European Convention of Human Rights and Fundamental Freedom does not create an absolute right to religious licence.

Sarva Dharma Sama Bhava does not add up to secularism. The spirit behind these words is universal tolerance. Secularism is essentially the separation of the church from the state. India never had a big enough church nor did it ever interfere in the running of the state. Islam on the other hand does not separate the temporal from the spiritual. The ultimate evidence of this was that the Caliph, or the representative of Prophet Muhammad, was the spiritual head and the temporal chief rolled into one. There was no dividing line between Caesar (the earthly ruler) and God.

In India, the practice during the British Raj was non-interference by the government in affairs of the religion. This was especially so after the so-called Sepoy Mutiny. It was only after Independence and the advent of vote bank politics that *Sarva Dharm Sama Bhava* began to be twisted in order to play one community against the other. Articles 25 to 30 were first introduced in 1946 with the intent of dissuading the Muslim League from insisting on Partition. Mysteriously, however, they survived in the draft constitution even after the country was torn asunder by Partition. The Marxists also call themselves secular. Their idea, however, is the abolition of religion. Karl Marx had considered religion to be the opium of the masses. In pursuance of his philosophy the Stalinists converted many a church, mosque and synagogue into shops, museums or offices across the Soviet Union.

Islam in Switzerland

In November 2009, the Swiss electorate in a referendum passed a Constitutional ban on minarets in their country. Switzerland has about three and a half lakh Muslims who have aroused a sense of threat amongst the rest of the country's citizens. The referendum was sponsored by a Conservative legislator Ulrich Schluer. The grounds cited were: the minaret is a political symbol against the integration of Muslims with the rest of the Swiss people. Secondly, this minority of today holds a threat of taking over not only the country but also most of Europe. The Swiss wished to resist the threat in order to preserve their culture. Ulrich Schluer in his forceful argument emphasised that London and Paris had Muslim ghettoes in their suburbs and the Swiss did not want that to happen in their country.

Schluer also found that Muslims practised double standards. In this context an academician asked: "How many churches have been constructed in Muslim countries in the last 60 years?" The answer was a big zero. In Christian countries, mosques have been built by the thousands during the same period. Muslims do not allow synagogues or temples in Islamic countries. They do not permit non-Muslims to set foot in Mecca and Medina but they move about with impunity in Bethlehem or the Vatican.

The association of Switzerland with Islam is rather recent. In 1970, there were fewer than 20,000 Muslims in the country. Today, with nearly five percent of the population, Islam is the country's second religion after Christianity. Being a highly federal polity, the policy towards immigrants varies from canton to canton. There is one policy in Geneva, another in Zurich and yet another in Neuchatel. In Geneva, wearing a headscarf by a government teacher is not permitted; the controversy over one instance is pending in the European Court of Human Rights in Strasbourg. In the Zurich canton, wearing a headscarf is tolerated and has never been a political issue. After some controversy, Muslim girls were exempted from learning to swim in public schools. Friday prayers are allowed to be organised in jails. Many of those in Swiss jails were inmates who had come from Kosovo and were drug dealers. One jail had 20 percent of its inmates from such a group. As a result, on Friday afternoons, this particular jail seemed more like a mosque than a prison!

Halal meat is another controversy. Switzerland prohibits the slaughter of animals before they are knocked unconscious. The Muslims of Neuchatel especially import halal meat from France. Another Muslim dispute in Switzerland is over graves and cemeteries, which in Islam must be eternal and not subject to recycling every 25 years. In Europe, the practice is to recycle as an answer to the shortage of land, but Islam does not permit removing the dead. This canton's Constitution prohibits isolated burial areas or private confessional cemeteries. Unless the Constitution is amended, this dispute cannot be resolved. In Zurich, there is a cantonal decree which also forbids separate burial areas. This decree was part of the struggle against religious discrimination. The mayor, then sympathetic to the Muslims, suggested that they collect funds and set up a separate private cemetery.

Despite the several cantonal differences of attitude to Muslims, this referendum threw up a national or confederal verdict that minarets should not be allowed. The problems being faced are a little different in other European countries as well as the USA, Britain, France, Holland, Italy, Norway, Spain, or Sweden. The Muslims in Britain have gone to the extent of demanding a separate Islamic parliament. In the state of Michigan in the USA, community leaders have alleged that the local public schools are taking away their youth from Islam. Little wonder that the late Prof Samuel Huntington (Amercian political scientist) had termed Muslim minorities as indigestible by non-Muslim societies. The real enemy of the USA was now the religiously driven militant Islam, this historian had reiterated.

Some five decades ago, Prof Wilfred Cantwell Smith (a Canadian Islamicist and scholar), in his seminal work *Islam in Modern History* had written: "The question of political power and social organization, so central to Islam, has in the past always been considered in yes-or-no terms. Muslims have either had political power or they have not. Never before have they shared it with others".

HISTORY

On Partition

There were two sides to the coin of Partition. One was that the Muslim community was well behind the Hindus as well as the other minorities. They were about one-third in number compared to the Hindus, so that if Independent India adopted universal adult franchise they would be out-numbered by lengths. Secondly, the Muslims were less educated. As a matter of long-term strategy, Islam has played down education from its early days of the 7th century. For the last thousand years, Hejaz as well as Caliphs had prohibited *ijtihad* (reinterpretation or change) and enforced *taqlid* (orthodoxy). The less educated a person, the fewer the questions he/she is likely to think up and ask, thus ensuring the perpetuity of the religion. Incidentally, women's studies were restricted to reading the Quran.

When the British came to India, instead of accepting English the Muslim clergy exhorted their followers to avoid the study of English and Western science. Sir William Hunter has made a lucid analysis of how and where the Muslim students fell back in the 19th century or even earlier. Then came the decision of Lt Governor of UP to make English the court language; the alternative was Hindi and Persian was abolished. Such measures, although rational, put the Muslims back. Their fear of diluting their identity was dearer to them than their development.

The other difficulty was that very few Muslims took to business and industry. The only exception were the Khojas, the Memons and the Bohras, all based in (the erstwhile) Bombay State. The Muslim elite of the rest of India were land-based, whether agricultural, farming vegetables or cultivating orchards but had very few factories. In short, the Hindus had the economic lead. Professor Timur Kuran, who teaches at the University of Duke USA, has explained at length the financial disadvantages of Islamic communities. He has focused on West Asia and how Islamic ordainments have kept the common folk economically backward. Imagine West Asia without petroleum! And imagine a business without banking and lending without interest!

The Viceroy had called an all-India election towards end of 1945 and early 1946. By that time, Jinnah's speech preceding the passing of the Pakistan resolution on 23 March 1940 at the Lahore session of the Muslim League, was humming in virtually all Muslim ears in India. Incidentally, Jinnah deliberately made Fazlur Rahman of Bengal sign the resolution. Rahman was a popular, prominent peasant leader of the eastern wing of what eventually became East Pakistan and now Bangladesh. Jinnah's espousal of the Two Nation Theory is very briefly stated here:

> The Hindus and Muslims have different religious philosophies, social customs and literatures. They neither

intermarry nor interdine and, indeed, they belong to two
different civilizations which are based mainly on conflicting
ideas and conceptions. Their views on life are different. It
is also quite clear that Hindus and Muslims derive their
inspiration from different sources of history. They have
different epics and different heroes in different episodes.
Very often the hero of one is a foe of the other so their
victories and defeats overlap.

History has presented to us many examples, such as the
union of Great Britain and Ireland. We know that the
history of the last 1,200 years has failed to achieve unity,
and have witnessed, during the ages India always divided
into Hindu India and Muslim India. The termination of
the British regime will be a worse disaster. Muslim India
cannot accept any constitution which must necessarily result
in a Hindu majority government. If Hindus and Muslims
are brought together under a democratic system, it can only
mean Hindu Raj. Muslims are not a minority; Muslims are
a nation according to any definition, and they must have
their homelands, their territory and their state.

As Dr Rafiq Zakaria (Indian politician and Islamic scholar)
put it: All through his younger years Jinnah showed no interest
in the Muslims. He was then all for the Congress; it was its
non-communal nationalism which enthused him.

When he was a young man, Jinnah worked for Hindu-
Muslim unity and made every attempt to see that the Congress
and the League presented a united front. He assured the British
that they need not be unduly perturbed as its terms of the
Lucknow Pact, if implemented, would help them as well. He

welcomed the declaration made by the British government on 20 August 1917, which assured Indians that "the policy of His Majesty's Government with which the Government of India are in complete accord, is that of the increasing association of self-governing institutions with a view to the progressive realization of responsible government in India as an integral part of the British Empire". To give effect to it, the new Secretary of State Edward Montague visited India in the winter of that year. He, along with Viceroy Lord Chelmsford, conferred with the leaders of different schools of political thought to try and find a consensus on the future constitutional advance. Of all the politicians whom Montague met, he was most impressed by Jinnah. He recorded this in his diary: "Young, perfectly mannered, impressive looking, armed to the teeth with dialectics, and insistent upon the whole of his scheme...."

Muslim League Accelerated Assam Immigration

What happened in Darrang district on 23 September 2021 whereby two alleged infiltrators were killed was sad but reflected the historic agony of the Assamese people. Under the Government of India Act of 1935, provincial governments were formed by political parties. Soon enough, Sir Muhammad Saadulla of the Muslim League became the premier. In the 1937 elections, the League led by MA Jinnah was disappointed with its meagre winnings in UP, the largest province. Talk of a distinctly separate Muslim holy land began in seriousness.

The idea was first concretely mooted by the poet Mohammad Iqbal who presided over the 1930 Muslim League session at Allahabad. A few years later, a Cambridge University scholar Chaudhry Rehmat Ali worked out a theoretical note and innovated the name Pakistan, the land of the pure. Jinnah's idea was that five provinces should form the holy land including Assam, Bengal, North West Frontier, Punjab and Sind. Balochistan came in later. From the Muslim majority angle, Assam appeared touch and go to Jinnah, although the Hindu impression was that they had a clear majority. Premier Saadulla got down to the business of facilitating as many east Bengali Muslims as could come across and settle in Assam. A whispering campaign was started that the Adivasis were not really Hindus but worshipped animals or were Christian. There was thus a race to somehow prove that there were more Muslims in Assam than Hindus.

In the course of a discussion at Shillong in 1945, Viceroy Lord Wavell noted in his diary that while the reason for the encouragement of this migration was officially justified as being to grow more food, the real object was to increase Mohammadans (as recorded by BK Nehru in his book *Nice Guys Finish Second*). The tale of illegal migrants into Assam is an old one told by all observers but swept under the carpet by the Congress party and its Muslim supporters. Other distinguished Muslims like Sheikh Mujibur Rahman and late Pakistan PM Zulfikar Ali Bhutto openly expressed the view that without Assam, the economy of East Pakistan could not be sustained.

The entire episode is heartrending for those who care for Assam. The writer has often visited the state and seen all its tea-growing sub-districts. He was there for ten days during the 1983 elections, which were boycotted by those who loved Assam. In many of the assembly constituencies, the voting was pathetically low although the then Hiteswar Saikia government had ensured perfect law and order. Most of the electoral offices in the heartland constituencies and the booths therein were manned by men flown in from other states. Nevertheless, for five days the Assamese districts seemed as dead as graveyards.

Quoting from *The Hindustan Standard*, a well-patronised Kolkata daily of those days, Dr Rajendra Prasad in his book *India Divided* stated: "It is sad but by no means improbable that in another 30 years Sibsagar district will be the only part of Assam in which an Assamese will find himself at home".

The Census Report of 1941 completes the story with a short but significant sentence: "The most noticeable rise in the Muslim population is in Assam, and once again represents migration from Mymensingh and east Bengal generally". This policy of colonisation of Assam by the Muslims of Bengal was continued under the joint auspices of the Muslim League ministries of Sir Saadulla in Assam and Nazimuddin in Bengal, as the following Bengal Government communique published in the press in the last week of October 1944 shows. It goes on to quote the Census Report of 1941: "The Government of Assam in their resolution dated 21 June 1940 prohibited settlement of land with persons coming from outside the province after 1 January 1938". The Bengal Legislative Council went on to appeal to the Governor to ask for the Viceroy's intervention in Assam.

Dr Rajendra Prasad quoted retired SP Desai, ICS, writing in *The Hindustan Standard* of December 1944: 'Every day new bamboo sheds and temporary huts are springing up in the reserves. I found that the immigrants absolutely ignore the local officers. The few Nepali graziers and Assamese Pamuas finding no protection from anywhere give "duhai" in the name of the King-Emperor'. Verily the cup of humiliation for the Assamese was full.

The Indira Gandhi government in collaboration with the then Assam CM Hiteswar Saikia suppressed the people of Assam and their sentiments. They continued to protest and agitate but to no avail. As if to rub salt on their wounds, the Central government passed the pernicious Illegal Migrants (Determination by Tribunals) Act in 1983. Hereby, in Assam the onus of proving that a particular person is an infiltrator rested with his complainant or the government of Assam, not on the suspect. The Foreigners Act of 1946, whereby the onus of proving his bonafides is on the suspect, continued to apply to all other states in India. The only exception made was Assam to help out the illegal migrants. When travelling from Guwahati to Shillong, one does not spontaneously realise when one has crossed from Assam to Meghalaya. Yet, in the latter state, the central law was the old 1946 Act! Such was the discrimination against the Assamese people.

Recalling Ambedkar

The Taliban, after having taken Afghanistan, training its guns on Islamabad is an ominous portent. Evidently the Mujahideen intend to cross the Indus in strength. Could it be that they intend to cross the Ichhogil canal, which is on the Indo-Pak border? If it were to be so, what would be India's answer? Not too long ago, the way the captured Pakistani terrorist of 26/11 (the 2008 jihadi terror attack on Mumbai), Ajmal Kasab, was tried like an ordinary criminal was an indication that the then regime and its secular fundamentalism were themselves a grave threat to the nation's security. Normally, a sovereign state would have treated Kasab as an enemy of the state, given him a summary trial and executed him. With the Muslim League a coalition partner of the then ruling UPA, with known jihadi sympathisers in the government, the UPA regime could hardly have been expected to move heaven and earth in order to resist a Talibani invasion.

India must fall back on its own nationalist ideology, that of

Hindutva. Rather than recalling Veer Savarkar's definition, it would be better to take the help of Dr BR Ambedkar's version of the patriotic ideology. For one, the acceptability of what Babasaheb wrote would be much higher across the classes and castes of India. For another, what he wrote was issue-specific and not merely in the realm of concept.

Ambedkar's viewpoint was supported by Qaid-e-Azam Jinnah. While proposing the Pakistan Resolution at the Lahore session of the Muslim League, the Qaid had said how and why Hindus and Muslims could not co-exist in the same country. Ambedkar's was not unilaterally a Hindu proposition; in his words: "That the transfer of minorities is the only lasting remedy for communal peace is beyond doubt" (Vol 8, *Writings and Speeches*, Govt of Maharashtra). Dr Ambedkar not only endorsed the Partition and an exchange of populations but also analysed in detail the geopolitical, the military and the financial implications of the separation. He admitted that India would have no natural land frontier especially in the north. He, however, argued in his book *The Partition of India* which he wrote immediately after Jinnah's historic Lahore resolution of 1940, that the deficiency could be offset by creating fortifications that might be far more impregnable than natural barriers.

Coming to the armed forces, Babasaheb pointed out that the fighting forces available for the defence of pre-Partition India mostly hailed from areas which were to become Pakistan. As things stood, India could not be defended without the help of the Pakistani provinces. Recruitment was based on the arbitrary theory that some communities were martial while others did not have fighting qualities. Perhaps the inadvertent effect of this excuse was that the Indian infantry was numerically dominated by Punjabi Muslims and Pathans. How far could Hindus depend upon these gatekeepers to hold the gates and protect the freedom of India? This was the question raised by Ambedkar. He went on to ask: "If a Muslim country were to invade India, would these gatekeepers stop the invaders or would they open the gates and let them in?"

Moreover, it was doubtful that a regiment of Muslims would accept the authority of Hindu officers if placed under them. In 1919, the Khilafat movement, led by the Ali brothers, had endorsed the Islamic viewpoint that a Muslim soldier would be justified in not resisting a Muslim invader. This view was subsequently endorsed by the Muslim League. Ambedkar concluded this problem lucidly: "Hindus have a difficult choice to make—to have a safe army or a safe border. If they desired to have a readymade safe border they would have to insist on Muslims remaining a part of India. On the other hand, if the Muslims go out, India would at least have a safe army". Which is better for the Hindus, he asked? Should the Muslims be without and against or should they be within and against. Ambedkar preferred the former.

The financial issues that Dr Ambedkar raised were equally important. He discovered that the dominantly Muslim provinces contributed less than 14 percent of the revenue to the central exchequer which contrasted with 85 percent contributed by the dominantly Hindu areas. At the time 43 percent of the total central government revenue was spent on the army, which comprised a dominant majority of Muslim soldiers. Babasaheb's conclusion was that the Hindus were paying for employing Muslim soldiers. He called this a paradox that fully justified the Partition.

As a member of the depressed classes, Babasabeb felt discriminated against and wished to change his faith. If he joined Islam or Christianity, he would go out not only from the Hindu religion, but also be out of the Hindu culture. To him, the consequences of conversion were also important. In his words: Conversion to Islam or Christianity would denationalise the depressed classes. If they went to Islam the number of Muslims would be doubled and the danger of Muslim domination also would become real. If they turned to Christianity, the numerical strength of Christians would go up to five to six crores. It would help to strengthen the hold of the British on this country ((Vol 17, *Writings and Speeches*).

Reliving the Era of Jaziya

Jaziya was conceived as a truce in the jihad between *momins* (believers in Islam) and *kafirs* (those who do not accept Islam). A demand for Rs 60 lakhs in *jaziya* was reported to have been made from the Hindus of Datagram in NWFP in June 2009. In the same year, 35 Sikh families were made homeless in Swat valley because they could not pay the demand of Rs 5 crore by the Taliban. Sad as these incidents are, they are tiny episodes in the vast epic of *jaziya* in the time of Prophet Muhammad.

Caliph Umar ibn Al-Khattab, who reigned between 634-44 AD, dictated a covenant whereby the resident Jews and Christians had to pay tribute to the Muslim rulers if they wished to survive with their respective faiths.

The inspiration of the covenant was founded upon a direct injunction of the Quran: "Make war upon those whom scriptures have not been given (the people of the Book)... until they pay tribute (*jaziya*) out of their hand, and they be humbled (page 248, *Dictionary of Islam* by Thomas Patrick Hughes, London, 1885). This was taken from Surah IX, Ayat

29 (*Quran* by A Yusuf Ali, 1934, Lahore). It says "Wage war until they pay the *jaziya* with willing submission and feel themselves subdued".

The Hanafi School of Islamic jurisprudence prescribed conversion or death to everyone other than the people of the Book namely Jews, Sabians and Christians. Notwithstanding this, the Muslim rulers in India extended the tribute or poll tax to Hindus. Evidently, this was done to meet economic compulsions of raising revenue. Otherwise, Hindus should be the last to be included considering the abhorrence of Islam for idolaters. *Jaziya* was introduced in India in 712 AD when Mohammed bin Qasim conquered Sind.

The poll tax continued to be levied by all Muslim rulers until Akbar abolished the practice in 1564. His great grandson Aurangzeb reimposed the vexatious levy in 1679. *Jaziya* ended with the advent of British rule. Jawaharlal Nehru, the friend of Muslims, could not have brought back a poll tax but he did introduce the Haj subsidy. His government legislated the Haj Committee Act, 1959. Its Article 14 deals with the subsidy, which includes any sum allotted by the central government or any state government to the Haj Fund. Nehru celebrated this bestowal by printing the word Haj on the normal currency notes signed by the then RBI Governor HVR Iyengar.

The central budget for 2005-06 provided Rs 25 crores for the fund. In the budget for 2009, the subsidy provision stood at Rs 413 crores. Prof Shri Ram Sharma, the doyen of historians in Lahore, wrote in 1940 that Akbar's gesture of 1564 had created a common citizenship for all his subjects, Hindus and Muslims alike. Aurangzeb reversed this visionary step until the British took over. Nehru reintroduced the policy of discrimination through the Haj subsidy, which presumably would help the Hajis to reach *jannat* (heaven). He, however, left all other fellow citizens, whether Hindus or Christians or others to their own devices for the pursuit of salvation.

The helpless Sikhs in Pakistan in 2009 were left with three options: either flee Swat valley if they could, embrace Islam or get killed. Right from the time of Nehru-Liaquat Pact of 1950, the Indian government has failed to come to the succour of the minorities, either in Pakistan or Bangladesh. In any case, the problem of minorities is not confined to the subcontinent. Eastern Europe was also affected for centuries. Eventually, a committee of the League of Nations, headed by the former Indian Viceroy Lord Curzon in 1923, concluded that an exchange of populations was the only lasting solution. In the event a whole new procedure of evaluating land, property, rights and duties of the migrating people was developed in detail. Thereafter, millions changed their countries from Turkey to Greece and from Greece to Turkey; similarly there was an exchange of Bulgarian Christians with the Turkish Muslims.

Muhammad Ali Jinnah and other leaders of the Muslim League right up to early 1947 proposed an exchange of populations between Hindustan and the emerging Pakistan. Gandhi and Nehru turned a deaf ear and the League had to eventually give up its proposal. When they got their homeland on 14 August 1947, they unilaterally began the ethnic cleansing of Hindus and Sikhs; the process was slower in the eastern wing. Surely, it is overdue that the Indian government wakes up and saves the minorities of the neighbouring countries; Pakistan has only a few lakhs left while their numbers in Bangladesh have come down to 8 percent.

A Flawed Partition

Of all the many scholars, historians and journalists who have written on the Partition, no one has fully dealt with the proposals put forth by the Muslim League. For example, the League leaders earnestly wanted an exchange of populations. The *Dawn*, a daily founded by Qaid-e-Azam Jinnah, in its columns through 1946-47, repeatedly carried the statements of his colleagues. The journal was published from Delhi until Partition and then moved to Karachi, from where it continues to be published.

While addressing the League legislators in Patna on 8 April 1945, Sir Feroz Khan Noon, who later became Prime Minister of Pakistan, threatened to re-enact the murderous orgies of Genghis Khan and Halaqu Khan if non-Muslims took up an obstructive attitude against population exchange. Ismail Chundrigar, who also eventually rose to be prime minister, had said in the same context that the British had no right to hand over Muslims to a people over whom "they had ruled for 500 years". Mohammad Ismail, a leader from Madras had declared that the Muslims of India were in the midst of a jihad. Shaukat Hayat Khan, son of the Punjab Premier, Sir Sikandar Hayat, had threatened a rehearsal of what the Muslims would eventually do to the Hindus. The point that came through clearly was that transfer of populations was an integral part of the demand for Pakistan.

Khan Iftikhar Hussain of Mamdot, president of the Punjab Muslim League, had said that the exchange of population offered a very practical solution for the problem of the Muslims (*Dawn*, 3 December 1946). Pir Ilahi Bux, a Sindhi leader, had said that he welcomed an exchange of population for the safety of the minorities, as it would put an end to all communal disturbances. This, too, was reported by *Dawn* on 4 December 1946. So also felt Raja Ghazanfar Ali, who later became Pakistan's envoy to New Delhi. The *Dawn* of 19 December 1945 reported his having asked for the alteration of the population map of India.

At a press conference which he addressed in Karachi on 25 November 1946, Jinnah had reiterated his anxiety by stating that the exchange of population question must be taken up immediately by the central as well as provincial governments. The issue was so much on the mind of the Muslim leaders that in the *Dawn* dated 3 December 1946, the Sind Premier Ghulam Hussain Hidayatullah offered to provide land for the Mohajirs from UP.

The idea of *hijrat* (migration) came more naturally to the Muslims than others. Prophet Muhammad himself had set the example by migrating from Mecca to Medina. By 1920, it was being realised that the Khilafat movement despite being led by

Gandhi and Maulanas Mohammad Ali and Shaukat Ali, would fail to save the Caliph from being dethroned in Turkey. There was then little hope of India again becoming a *Dar-ul-Islam* (a land ruled by Islam) which it was considered to be until 1858 when Bahadur Shah Zafar was the last Mughal emperor. As a consequence, several lakh Muslims undertook a *hijrat* to Afghanistan around 1915, and 20,000 of them actually succeeded in settling in that country.

The Muslim League leaders must also have been aware that in pursuance of the Turko-Bulgarian Convention of 1913, Muslim Bulgarians were resettled in Turkey and many non-Muslim Turks were transferred to Bulgaria. Such an exchange of population took place on a much larger scale between Turkey and Greece under the Treaty of Lausanne signed on 30 January 1923 under the auspices of the League of Nations. Incidentally, former Viceroy Lord Curzon presided over the population committee of the League of Nations. Former Vice-Chancellor Mujeeb of the Jamia Milia Islamia had an interesting experience which he narrates in his book *Islamic Influence on Indian Society*. At the UN General Assembly Session in 1949, he happened to be seated next to the Turkish representative. Seeing Mujeeb's name, the Turkish representative at once asked, "Are there still any Muslims in India?" He thought that the subcontinent had been divided between Muslims and Hindus, with all Muslims on one side and all Hindus on the other.

Prof M Mujeeb in his book *Indian Muslims* clarified the issue: "If Mr Jinnah was sincere in regarding the Muslims as a separate nation and demanding separate territory for them, it was his obvious and inescapable moral duty to define the boundaries of Pakistan. He should also have realised that a transfer of populations would be inevitable".

The demand for a transfer of populations is clearly mentioned in the official record called *The Transfer of Power 1942-47* by Nicholas Mansergh. Jinnah stated: "I am not fighting for Muslims believe me when I demand Pakistan. Pakistan and Hindustan alone will mean freedom to both Hindus and Muslims". He went on with a direct reference to the disturbances when he said: "The exchange of populations will have to be considered seriously".

In his book *Pakistan or the Partition of India*, Dr BR Ambedkar recognised the problem of the transfer of population and went on to quote its solution in Europe. He had studied the experience of Bulgaria, Greece and Turkey. He stressed that the exchanges had worked and recommended their repetition in the Indian subcontinent.

Had there been
no Pakistan

Most of us yearn for an undivided India but none of us tarries a while to ponder what would have happened had there been no partition. The affairs of state and society have to be guided by reality and not be driven by sentiments. The country today has a 15 percent Muslim population. Just look at the way all political parties except one are lured by the minority vote. Can we forget how a former prime minister of India whose family was driven out of West Punjab, not too long ago, had declared: "Muslims must have the first claim on India's resources." He appointed the Sachet Committee with the express intention of giving Muslims a preferential share in the country's resources. Another party promised to evict squatters on waqf lands, completely ignoring the fact that the properties in question are actually Hindu, forcibly snatched by the Muslim invaders from Hindus.

Early in 1983, a Lahore journalist had interviewed Ayatollah Khomeini of Iran for a special feature in anticipation of Pakistan Day of that year. Towards the end, the interviewer asked the Iranian leader's opinion on Jinnah. The Ayatollah was generous in his praise but did not fail to say that the Quid lacked vision. If Jinnah had the foresight, Khomeini said, he would have waited and in due course the whole of India would have been in Muslim hands. Instead, Jinnah settled for only two-fifths of the subcontinent.

If India were undivided, the Muslim population today would be about 40 percent. It would be pertinent to recall that in 1947 the Muslim numbers were 25 percent and evidently we could not co-exist. While sponsoring the Pakistan Resolution Jinnah had said: 'Hindus and Muslims belong to two different civilizations which are based mainly on conflicting ideas and conceptions. To yoke together two such nations under a single state, one as a numerical minority and the other as a majority, must lead to growing discontent and final destruction of any fabric that may be so built up for the government of such a state.'

Chaudhry Khaliquzzaman, who succeeded Jinnah as President of the Muslim League, has written in his book, *Pathway to Pakistan*, "Democracies are the creatures of numbers and the Muslims in India had both numbers and geographical advantages. So far as I could see they would never be prepared to accept that status (minority) but would fight to the last man to avert it. The consequences would be perpetual bitterness, disturbances and fights within India. Then why should we not separate?"

These views were a carry forward from what other leaders had said before. One might go back to Sir Syed Ahmad Khan who in 1887 while delivering a speech at Lucknow had said: "I object to every Congress in any shape or form whatever, which regards India as one nation, on account of its being based on wrong principles". Mohammad Iqbal, the composer of "*Sare jaban se achha, Hindustan hamara*" had subsequently switched to "*Muslim hain hum, vatan hai sara jahan hamara*". In the 1930 session of the Muslim League at Allahabad, Iqbal had said: "I would like to see Punjab, North-West Frontier Province (NWFP), Sind and Baluchistan amalgamated into a single state, self-governing within the British Empire or without the British Empire. The formation of a consolidated north-west Indian Muslim state appears to be the final destiny of the Muslims, at least of north-west India".

These ideological statements of Jinnah, Khaliquzzaman, Sir Syed and Iqbal show that separatism flowed in the bloodstream of Islam. Even when in Mughal times the Muslim population was perhaps only 10 percent, the community was happy because they believed that the empire was a *Darul- Islam*. The biggest difference of opinion between the Taliban and the rest of Pakistan is whether the Sharia would prevail or would be diluted by any other system of law. That is also the reason the former Zardari government of Pakistan had to concede the application of Sharia in the Swat Valley of the country's northwest, in order to obtain a truce with the Taliban, which today controls Afghanistan.

Despite there being much fewer Muslims in the UK, their orthodox *ulema* (clergy) have gone to the extent of demanding a separate Islamic parliament.

An Islamic state revolves around a few parameters as listed by Maulana Maududi and recounted by Jamia Millia vice-chancellor M Mujeeb in his book *Indian Muslims*. Society is divided between *momins* (believers) and *kafirs* (infidels); the latter must pay *jaziya* or tax for being allowed to stay alive and *khiraj* or land revenue. Muslims have to pay *zakaat* (contribution) and *ushr* (a tax on produce from the land). Sharia should prevail whereby *Dar-ul-qaza* (a Muslim magistrate or judge) would dispense justice, according to Islamic law, of course. The first charge on the state revenue would be for the welfare of Muslims.

Don't we see all these features already in operation in areas where Muslims are in a majority, even if they are deviously applied? Articles 25 to 30 of the Constitution of India discriminate in favour of Muslims. The Haj subsidy, abolished after 2014, was only the tip of the iceberg. It financed Muslim institutions like madarsas, universities like AMU, *wakfs* et al through Indian taxpayers' money; these constitute an indirect *jaziya. Dar-ul-qazas* already function in certain areas, though surreptitiously. Innumerable temples that were converted into mosques are still in Muslim hands. Is this not already a rehearsal for an Islamic state?

Amazing Tales as History

The *Rediscovery of India* by Meghnad Desai begins with the advent of Vasco Da Gama. The presumption is that the Portuguese adventurer inaugurated the contact of India with the rest of the globe. That Mohammed-bin-Qasim arrived in Sind in 712 AD, Mahmud of Ghazni invaded India seventeen times, Mohammed Ghori's face-off with Prithviraj Chauhan of Delhi in the last decade of the 12th century and whoever else came to India before that, in between and after, is discounted. Why this partiality for the white man or the European? In Desai's own words: "My argument in this book is that many of India's problems lie in a flawed understanding of its own history. Both nationalist and British historians have contributed to this process. Like a patient with a psychological problem, India needs to revisit its birth traumas as a nation. The remedy may be quite radical if one is to rearrange the patient's psyche so she/he can be well again".

Whether it is India that is the psychological patient or the author himself is something that needs to be gone into. The outstanding fundament of Islam is that Allah is the only God. How then can his *momin* or faithful consider having a religious debate with the *kafirs* or non-believers? Incidentally, the word *kafir* has evolved out of the word *kufr* or blasphemy. On page 30 of his book, Desai praises Akbar's initiative of marrying Hindu princesses as a sign of tolerance. But this tradition did not extend to reciprocation in the form of marriage of Muslim princesses to Rajput kings. The Mughal household had plenty of unmarried princesses. For example, all the three daughters of Shah Jahan—Jahan Ara, Roshan Ara and Gauhar Ara remained unmarried.

On one page Desai states that by 1909 the Congress had failed to construct a narrative of Indian nationhood which was inclusive of the diverse religions. He has obviously overlooked the 1887 Congress resolution passed under the presidentship of Badruddin Tyabji that 'no subject of Mahomedan interest could be discussed by the party without the prior unanimous concurrence of the Muslim representatives'. On another page the author states that in 1940 Jinnah was not bargaining for a separate nation state; he was brokering for minority rights. Has Lord Meghnad read Jinnah's presidential speech at the March 1940 Lahore session of the League? Jinnah had stated in that speech in no ambiguous terms: "The Hindus and Muslims belong to two different civilizations which are based mainly on conflicting ideas and conceptions. To yoke together two such nations under a single state must lead to growing discontent and final destruction of any fabric" (*Constitutional and Political History of Pakistan* by Hamid Khan, Oxford University Press).

In his book *The Rediscovery of India* Desai has referred

to Sir Aga Khan, but has done so incorrectly. He is stated to have met the British statesman Lord Morley in 1907, whereas the fact was that Aga Khan led a delegation of 35 eminent Muslims to Viceroy Lord Minto at Shimla in October 1906 and had, *inter alia*, asked for separate electorates. Has Desai had the opportunity to read the letter dated 24 January 1888 by Syed Ahmed Khan addressed to Badruddin Tyabji wherein the former wrote, "I object to every Congress in any shape or form whatever which regards India as one nation on account of its being based on wrong principles, viz. that it regards the whole of India as one nation. Probably you will not like my ideas and, therefore, I hope you will excuse me for venturing to write so much".

Why has the author overlooked or ignored so many scholars? The American scholar Wilfred Cantwell Smith wrote, "It was primarily the Indian Muslims who were responsible for the emergence of the new state (Pakistan) and, therefore, also for the consequent position of their community on the Indian side of the frontier. The Pakistanis followed and accepted, but the Indian Muslims led and created". Dr Aziz Ahmad wrote, "Jinnah did not lead, but was led by the Muslim consensus. His role was that of a sincere and clear-headed lawyer who could formulate and articulate in precise terms what his client really wanted". Prof IH Qureshi's *The Muslim Community* contended that those who expected Muslims to accept their minority status were deplorably ignorant of the psychology of the community. Muslims were bound to claim to be a nation by themselves.

Prof SM Ikram wrote that the ground for Muslim separation was prepared when Islam entered the subcontinent.

Prof Francis Robinson of England had written that UP's Muslims were at the heart of the Muslim separation supported by some Bombay-based co-religionists like Jinnah. M Mujeeb, former Vice-Chancellor of Jamia Millia, has produced a seminal work about the Muslim League. In the elections held in 1946 it secured the majority of the Muslim seats. This showed that the Muslims were overwhelmingly in favour of Pakistan. Chaudhary Khaliquzzaman, who succeeded Jinnah as the League president had asked: "Would the Muslims ever agree to a minority status? Would Islam tolerate 100 million Muslims being cut adrift?"

Despite leaving out so many sources, Meghnad Desai has the audacity to write, "Lack of a single story of why India should be considered a single nation was at the heart of Partition of India". Contrast this statement with what historian Sardar KM Panikkar had to say in his famous *Survey of Indian History*: "Indian history is of necessity, predominantly the history of the Hindu people...the Hindus still constitute over eighty percent of her population. Besides, what is distinctly Indian has so far been Hindu".

Recall the 'Great Calcutta Killings'

Not many Indians remember or know that on 16 August 1946 the bloodiest and the biggest state-sponsored riots in the country's history began. The riots took place in Calcutta, the capital of undivided Bengal, whose premier was Huseyn Shaheed Suhrawardy the Muslim League leader in the assembly. Incidentally, he later became prime minister of Pakistan.

August 16 was planned by the League led by Jinnah to launch a 'Direct Action Day' to convince the British that Hindus and Muslims could not coexist in the same country and, hence, India must be partitioned. The tactical manifesto was distributed to the League activists; it had 23 points as reproduced by Justice GD Khosla in his famous work *Stern Reckoning* (Oxford University Press India, 1949). A few of the points read as follows: "Destroy Hindus and drive all Hindus out of India. All transport should be used for battle against Hindus. Hindu women and girls should be raped, kidnapped and converted into Muslims from October 18, 1946. Hindu culture should be destroyed". The Calcutta District Muslim League of 13 August 1946 published an elucidation of the programme quoted above. It clarified that the 'Direct Action Day' was to be conducted in the name of the Quran, the holy month of Ramzan, Battle of Badr and the Holy Prophet.

On 22 August, Bengal Governor Sir Frederick Burrows wrote a detailed report to Viceroy Lord Wavell on what came to be known as the Great Calcutta Killings. To quote Burrows for 16 August: "The trouble had already assumed the communal character which it was to retain throughout. At the time it was mainly in the northern half of the city. Later reports indicate that the Muslims were in an aggressive mood from early in the day and that their processions were well-armed with *lathis*, iron rods and missiles". To quote Burrows for 17 August: "This tour convinced me that the reports that I had received of the seriousness of the situation had erred on the side of underestimation. I observed very great damage to property and streets littered with corpses. I can honestly say that parts of the city on Saturday morning were as bad as anything I saw when I was with the Guards on the Somme (the bloodiest battle of WWI fought in Belgium wherein the total casualties were estimated to be 12,65,000 soldiers). The feeling was entirely communal".

The highlight of August 18 in the Governor's letter was: "I made another tour of inspection, this time with the Army Commander and the chief minister, covering large areas in the south and south-east of the city which I had not visited before. The chief minister showed an exasperating preoccupation with the sufferings undergone by members of his own community". The slaughter over the first few days was so widespread that

Burrows could not give any authoritative casualty figures. Guided mainly by hospital figures, he guessed 2,000 dead at the very least. But in the mayhem, most of the injured got nowhere near a hospital. In fact, no one was available to clear the dead bodies until "the Army came to my rescue on the basis of Rs 5 a body to volunteers", the Governor wrote.

The Statesman, then a British-owned daily, on 22 August wrote: "The group of incompetents, or worse, who owing to their office necessarily bear primary responsibility for the criminal carnage in Calcutta, a catastrophe of scope unprecedented in India's history, have been insufficiently seen or heard in these grim days. We mean the Ministry". BK Nehru, in his memoirs *Nice Guys Finish Second* (Viking 1997) commented: "This massacre of the Hindus and Sikhs by Muslims was well organized and directed personally by HS Suhrawardy".

Headlined "Calcutta's Ordeal", *The Statesman* on 20 August had written: "The origin of the appalling carnage and loss in the capital of a great Province, we believe the worst communal rioting in India's history, was a political demonstration by the Muslim League". The *Modern Review*, an eminent monthly of the time wrote in its September 1946 issue: "Soon the city was ablaze from North to South and from East to West. The Hindus of Calcutta gradually realised that denial of police aid was part of the programme. It was not as if there was not enough force at the disposal of the authorities. Armed police and Anglo-Indian armed sergeants were there in plenty, sitting idle and twiddling their thumbs. The situation soon became precarious for the Hindus all over Calcutta".

What MA Jinnah said, as quoted by Justice Khosla, was the most authoritative declaration on the killing: "What we have done today is the most historic act in our history. Never have we in the whole history of the League done anything except by constitutional methods and by constitutionalism. But now we are obliged and forced into this position. This day we bid goodbye to constitutional methods". This was so Machiavellian. Ironically, Jinnah had begun life as a barrister and had remained a constitutionalist for the greater part of his career. The political leaders of today are often ill-educated and also unscrupulous. For illustration, one may look at the instance of how the erstwhile J&K government went back on its own decision to earmark 100 acres for the use of the Amarnath pilgrims. Its coalition partner the People's Democratic Party (PDP) not only resigned but also incited the Valley to agitate against the decision.

A much worse example is the e-mail sent out by the Indian Mujahideen: "Hindus have no compassion in their religion. It is the duty of Muslims to wage a jihad against Hindu oppressors and it is the Hindu who is a terrorist". In this day and age, the e-mail invokes Islamic invaders like Ghauri and Ghaznavi to settle the score with Hindus. Imagine if people like this came anywhere near power, they may make the Great Calcutta Killings appear to be a mere fracas.

What is Fascism?

The celebration in the USA of Swami Vivekananda's hundredth birthday was yet another occasion when the secular fundamentalists were provoked to call the RSS and Vishwa Hindu Parishad—fascist. A meeting presided over by the well-known journalist (late) Kuldip Nayyar was held to dissuade the famous danseuse Ms Sonal Mansingh from going to Washington to present a dance item in connection with the celebration. In their view, their most decisive argument was that the organisers of the celebration were fascist. What they did not realise is that the word is not a political abuse that they think it is. Benito Mussolini, who initiated the fascist movement in March 1919 at Milan and founded the party called Partito Nazional Fascista in November 1921, eventually did die in defeat and disgrace. That is, however, too farfetched to be abusive; or, does the very word "fascist" denote political derogation? Perhaps that is reason enough to recapitulate what fascism is.

The word "fascio" means a bundle or a bunch implying unity. The movement was in response to the corruption, unemployment and the virtual economic collapse in Italy after World War I. The then prevailing socioeconomic conditions appeared to be ripe for a communist revolution and fascism was a nationalist answer to pre-empt a Red takeover. Marxism was looked upon as depicting "class conflict". Capitalism still carried the stigma of "class exploitation" and was, therefore, a non-starter as a popular programme. To be effective, the answer had to be something that would prove attractive to the peasants, the workers as well as to their unions. This was discovered in "class collaboration" as represented by fascism.

Prof Alfredo Rocco, the Minister of Justice in the Mussolini cabinet, set forth the gist of this new ideology in the course of a speech at Perugia in 1925. According to him, the society does not exist for the individual; it is the individual who has to exist for the society. Economic progress is a social interest and all classes of people should combine or collaborate to maximise production. The interests of the employers and the employed are identical. To ensure that this is practiced, there must be a system of state discipline over class conflicts. Strikes and lockouts were alike illegal and punishable by heavy fines, and in certain cases, by imprisonment.

Wherever possible, the employers and workers in each industry, trade or profession were organised together in syndical associates. In places where it was not possible to form such syndicates, the unions and the employers' associations remained but combined to form guilds to coordinate and ensure cordiality. If collective bargaining could not end disputes satisfactorily, they were referred to law courts assisted by experts. This is how class collaboration was conceptualised by the Fascist Party.

In practice, the economy was toned up by rearmament and public works. Soldiers were recruited in large numbers and so were workers in factories to produce arms. This would bring profits to the bourgeoisie who could then pay the proletariat well. Urban prosperity would increase demand for agricultural produce. What was left of the underemployed youth was absorbed by the armed forces. The promise to the whole nation was foreign conquests, which would bring booty. The Albanian adventure and the invasion of Abyssinia (now Ethiopia) were two endeavours to fulfill this promise until World War II took place.

Another example of the practice of fascism or class collaboration, albeit on a much more limited scale, was in Spain under General Franco. Neither the Italian nor the Spanish experience is widely known in any great detail in India. What the members of the intelligentsia are familiar with are the doings of Adolf Hitler and his Nazi Party, whose full name was National Socialist German Workers' Party. It was founded by Hitler and his six comrades in Munich in 1920. The economic deprivation in Germany was much greater than witnessed in Italy. The country paid an exorbitant price for its defeat in World War I. The runaway inflation as well as the worldwide Great Depression ignited by the crash in share prices on the Wall Street in New York in 1929 made matters hot for Germany. It was widely believed that the charismatic genius of Hitler and his programme of class collaboration, more or less on the lines of Mussolini's Italy, although on a far grander scale, saved the country from utter collapse and a communist takeover.

Unlike the Italian and Spanish examples, the Nazi Party was determined to exclude Jews from German life. They alleged that the Jewish leadership had betrayed the German nation during World War I and were to a large extent responsible for Germany's defeat. In their bid to exterminate the Jews, not only from Germany but also from the rest of Europe, the Nazis were estimated to have killed six million Jews in 1945. While General Franco confined himself to Spain, Benito Mussolini did attempt foreign conquests but his plans were nowhere as grandiose as Adolf Hitler's.

So much for fascism and its smaller as well as grander (Spanish and German) variations. But what is its ugly connection with politics in India? India is not Europe. The 2020s are not the 1930s. Socialism has expired, and lives only in the rhetoric of university campuses and some media chambers; and there is no fear of a communist takeover in India. There are economic challenges but no danger of financial collapse on the scale of pre-Hitlerite Germany. India's ethos has no record of imperialism and, therefore, no promise of foreign conquests would be credible. If an attempt is being made to compare the Jews of Germany and the Muslims of India, it is ridiculous. No one has accused the Muslims of betraying India, not even the BJP whose only contention is that there has been appeasement of Muslim whims and pampering of the community's leadership. The Muslim masses, unlike the Jews who were influential, are poor. All in all, to call any one a fascist in India is to talk nonsense.

MISCELLANEOUS

NCC Makes a Complete Person

As many as 114 of our universities have decided not only to introduce National Cadet Corps (NCC) but also allow the cadets exemption from one subject. In short, treat NCC as part of the curriculum. I believe this is a sterling step for building national character and should be extended to senior school students too.

The experiences inculcated in NCC contribute to one's character which remains until the end of one's life. I was in the artillery wing during my college days and the gun that was the focus of our training was the Second World War standard gun, the immediate predecessor of the Bofors howitzer. Our gun was called the 25 pounder because the shell weighed 25 pounds. It was operated by six cadets.

In artillery, the base unit was called the battery which had 60 gunners or cadets, and was commanded by a Major. There were two officers under him and several junior commissioned officers who began as jawans and could rise to the rank of Subedar Major. These JCOs were in charge of training us NCC cadets. Once in uniform, we forgot who was what, except cadets of the Second Bombay Battery and that one day we might be called upon to fight for India. We did not think of death, but as luck would have it one occurred during our December camp of a fortnight at Deolali, which is one of the country's major artillery centres. One day was selected for gun firing; the range was several kms away. We were taken in two 3-ton trucks usually used by the army for dragging the guns. Every gunner team of six cadets got to actually work a gun and every cadet got one chance to pull the trigger to send a 25 pounder shell flying away. The hope was that it would land on the target. A Major sat on a tree ahead of us to guide us where to aim.

The entire exercise took over four hours and it was then time to return. I was one of the cadets given a rifle to carry; some others were given some other lighter baggage. I was too tired to carry the rifle, yet the Cadet Sergeant insisted. I begged him to let me carry a pack of things and not the rifle which was a WWII .303 standard model. Eventually, the Sergeant took pity on a young tired boy of 15 and let me off. In the armed forces, one neither begs nor argues; one just obeys. Those carrying baggage were sent by the first truck while the cadets with rifles followed a few minutes later.

Halfway through, a senior cadet in our truck who happened to be standing noticed that the second truck had fallen to the side of the road, ten feet or so lower in the field. Our colleague shouted about the accident and asked the driver to turn back. We reached the spot in a few minutes; everyone jumped out to help. I was asked to stand in one place in case anything was required from our vehicle. The scene was worse than a one-sided battle. My heart went out to our injured colleagues; for no rhyme or reason so many were hurt. They were taken to hospital in our vehicle.

After five days, we were allowed to visit the hospital to see our injured colleagues for a total of five minutes. All except one had recovered quickly. Dinesh Pai was still not conscious and the nurse hinted that he may not survive. He died a few days later, we were informed on our return to Mumbai. We all felt sad but that is all. We took the death as a professional hazard of a soldier's life. This was a lesson I have remembered throughout my life. Once on a trip to Dibrugarh, flying by a four-engine Skymaster, we ran into a violent cyclone. For thirty-five minutes the plane did everything conceivable except break either of its wings. That is why it did not crash, I was later told. At one stage, the plane dropped in a 900-feet deep air pocket but fortunately came up again. Many of the passengers were crying, screaming, vomiting and what not. The person next to me was praying loudly. Two passengers had fainted. I kept recalling Deolali, consoling myself that one could die accidentally too, as Cadet Pai did.

When the Chinese invaded Arunachal Pradesh, I had no hesitation in volunteering. The question of death did not even occur to me. By being in the NCC, one quite unconsciously gets committed to the country above all. The spirit of discipline survives right through one's life, plus the lesson that the team is always greater than the player.

As has been said, the Battle of Waterloo was won on the playing fields of Eton (an elite English Public School). National Tabacco Company, the second biggest after ITC, could not have been revived but for my NCC experience. Recalcitrance by 2,400 workers had to be overcome in Kolkata.

Merit in Judges

There is a proposal at the highest level in the judicial world that merit must come first in the selection of judges. Without it, litigants will not be able to get justice. Who can differ with this proposal? Selection by merit also does justice to the bench.

How do we decide what merit is? More difficult would be the question of how to identify merit. The assessment of the prospective individual would have to be made in several stages. First, the individual's knowledge of law and jurisprudence has to be tested, if necessary by a private debate between two or three aspiring candidates, with a very senior person, preferably an advocate, supervising the debate. Thereafter, the more important aspect, as observed by a former litigant, is the impartiality of the potential judge.

Not being an expert, I hesitate to comment on this process. Nevertheless, I could fall back on my experience as a youngster while appearing for the Services Selection Board at Prayagraj as an example, where they chose commissioned officers for the army. For two full days, candidates had to answer written questions, as well as perform some exercises in writing. I could not understand the objective of this two-day long exercise, but did carry it out in all seriousness.

The third day was for medical tests and discussions. Medically, the Board found my knees knocked against each other. Very strictly speaking, such a person would be unsuitable for long marches. However, this deficiency got overlooked by the director. The final morning had physical tests like passing through tyres, surmounting obstacles and crossing rivulets by clutching ropes. I scored only 3 marks out of 75, while the next lowest performer obtained 26 out of 75. As a result, I had reconciled myself to having failed.

Yet, I received a call in the evening for the final interview, and was grilled for nearly forty minutes. Several other candidates finished their interviews after only three to five minutes. The subject of my repeated questioning was my ambition in life, which I refused to disclose right till the end. To my utter surprise, the Board passed me in the whole test. It also made me think subsequently that there was much more to the tests on paper than was obvious prima facie.

I cannot think of any other way to judge the impartiality of a potential judge other than psychiatric tests. Here, it bears iteration that one cannot overestimate the importance of impartiality. It is only an impartial judge, and by extension an impartial judiciary, that can protect the rights of all citizens, irrespective of their background. People seeking the help of courts to resolve their disputes or seeking justice for whatever wrong they feel has been done to them must have the confidence that the judges deciding their cases will act in a neutral manner.

Impartiality can be said to be the foremost criterion of merit when it comes to selection of judges.

While this quality must command universal allegiance, it has particular relevance for a country like ours, which is marked by a substantial degree of social and economic disparities arising out of our caste system and other circumstances. The idea of judicial impartiality must become central to our public discourse. Again, this needs constant reiteration because in recent times, some instances and trends in the judicial sphere in India have revealed some disquiet if not discontent over the functioning of their lordships.

Not too long ago, there was an instance of a former judge who is now a political activist, openly voicing his intense dislike for a particular caste. It is a moot point as to the fate of any litigant of that caste unlucky to have appeared before this judge. There have been instances reported of judicial corruption too. In May 2017, a Chief Justice of India-led seven-judge bench convicted a sitting High Court judge for contempt of court and sentenced him to six months imprisonment, which was a first in the history of Indian judiciary. This High Court judge had levelled corruption charges against 33 judges, 14 of the Supreme Court and 19 of the Madras High Court. While the judge in question was handed a prison sentence, the issue he had raised remains unanswered till date. It needs no genius to understand the effect corruption in the judiciary is likely to have on the people. There is a strange case of a former (now deceased) chief minister judged guilty by a special court judge of one state for possession of disproportionate assets and arrested after the case had dragged on for 18 years. He was released by a judge of the High Court of that state the very next year which did not bring any credit to the image of the judiciary in India. It also raises questions about the merit of those selected to deliver justice.

Some former judges have not minced words in stating that it is the faith of the people that sustains the judiciary. Now that one of its luminaries has opened up the debate on the need for merit to be the chief criterion in selecting judges, one hopes this matter will see closer scrutiny.

The Third Way Could be the Way Forward

Along with his Cabinet expansion, Prime Minister Narendra Modi introduced a Ministry of Co-operation in July 2021. Earlier, on a visit to the Amul Dairy district Anand in Gujarat, he had called this the third way; the Prime Minister probably meant limited corporations, partnerships/proprietorships and now also cooperatives.

Why are cooperatives, or cooperative institutions important? One, they enable the direct participation of people in entrepreneurial activity. Two, they involve the trust of the beneficiaries. The cooperative movement commands trust even in the developed West. An International Labour Organisation (ILO) report says that during the 2008 global financial crisis, cooperative banks reported only 7 percent of the total losses and write-offs in the Western banks. In contrast, banking giants like the Lehman Brothers suffered huge meltdowns. Cooperative banks form 20 percent of Europe's banking system. More than 60 percent Americans trust the country's credit union banks, as compared to commercial ones.

The Co-operative Societies Act was enacted in 1912. The Anand Milk Union Limited, which today is a global Indian brand by the name of Amul, was started in 1946 under the direction of Sardar Vallabhbhai Patel. Cooperative societies are working from New Zealand in the east to the USA in the west.

But in India they have a seminal role to play. Let us take the saga of Amul, the country's best known and most successful cooperative institution. Under Sardar Patel's initiative, dairy farmers of the then Kheda district of Gujarat organised themselves to form a dairy cooperative in order to directly undertake sale and processing of milk collected from member dairy farmers of the district.

Amul has made a world of difference not only to India's dairy farming, but also the country's socioeconomic life. Figures tell this story like nothing else. During the two decades between 1950 and 1970, milk production grew by a bare one percent annually; per capita availability of milk actually declined by an equivalent percentage in the same period. Various state governments in the decade of the 60s tried different strategies to develop dairying, including establishing dairies run by their own departments. Cattle colonies were set up to enhance milk production, but were concentrated in urban areas and not in the milk sheds or cattle-grazing zones.

It was Operation Flood implemented by the National Dairy Development Board (NDDB), which revolutionised dairy development in India. Beginning in 1970, the NDDB replicated Amul's successful model. Here, individual farmers are joined in village-level dairy cooperative societies (DCS), which in turn are joined in state-level marketing federations. The Amul pattern in each state has decentralised milk production by small milk producers, milk procurement by village-level dairy cooperative societies, centralised milk production by district-level unions and marketing of milk and milk products by the state federations.

Primary milk producers govern this entire federal cooperative structure to ensure that the higher tier organisations cater to the lower tiers and the gains at all levels flow back to the milk producers in significant measure. The Anand model enabled Operation Flood, making India the world's largest producer of milk at more than 100 million tonnes annually, valued at Rs 900 billion per year.

Milk today reaches more than 750 towns and cities of the country through the National Milk Grid Network. The number of women's cooperatives has grown significantly. The cooperative model has empowered them in ways that were inconceivable decades ago. Women dairy cooperatives, with further branching out into animal husbandry, are another success story of this movement.

The cooperative movement has seen one of its great successes in Maharashtra and Karnataka, particularly the former. In Maharashtra, the cooperative movement has been embraced by the states' rural and urban folk alike. It has also spawned across-the-board success in the production of sugar and in the banking sector. In rural Maharashtra, it is cooperative banks that hold sway and are the preferred banking institutions to deposit money. The cooperative movement in this state has also morphed into the political sphere. The sugar cooperatives in the state have become the prima donna of political influence and power.

One cannot also deny that many cooperative banks have

floundered or are struggling. This is because they have shied away from professionalising their management. Instead, many have opted for what is sometimes derisively referred to as the "Lalu model of management". In other words, family members or cronies have been appointed in the top decision-making posts. But this does not diminish the importance of the cooperative movement.

This third way—the cooperative approach—can enable a farmer of even a couple of hectares of land-holding, or his urban counterpart, to be a partner in entrepreneurship. The apex cooperative and its management need to be honest as well as imaginative. Depending on the product, it can be a manufacturing or a marketing exercise, while the cooperatives at the field level would supply the input, like milk in the case of Amul. It is a marvellous idea for a country with a large population and comparatively little land. The proprietorship/partnership model is the second way for the middle rung of entrepreneurs, while the first way is of the limited company model.

Agriculture Better
for Eastern India

Prime Minister Modi has recently suggested to the country's farmers 35 new and varied types of vegetations that are of high yield or high value, or both. Among the crops the prime minister has suggested for future agricultural development are chickpea, wilt and sterility mosaic-resistant pigeonpea, early maturing variety of soya bean, disease-resistant varieties of rice, biofortified varieties of wheat, pearl millet, maize, quinoa, buckwheat, winged bean, faba bean, etc.

Apart from prospects of India's agricultural growth, this suggestion could just be the answer for a prosperous eastern India as well. In a recently published book titled *Had Patel been Prime Minister*, this author has delved into how Sardar Vallabhbhai Patel, had he been the country's prime minister instead of Jawaharlal Nehru, would have treated the issue of India's economic development, particularly that of eastern India. Patel had novel ideas. He would have promoted eastern India distinctly for farming and agriculture. In his time, the

35 new crops suggested by our current prime minister might not have been known. Yet, the concept that there are plants that are drought resistant, inimical to pests or excessive rain or flooding was indeed known.

The thrust of this submission is to reiterate an important aspect of Sardar Patel's outlook. He was from a farmer's family and well acquainted with farmers' issues and problems. In fact, he organised and led the Bardoli Satyagraha as a farmers' revolt against excessive taxes in the face of financial difficulties in the year of 1928. The movement made Sardar Patel a national leader. Prior to his political career and role in the country's independence movement, Vallabhbhai was also a prominent lawyer in Ahmedabad and not unfamiliar with industry. Moreover, he was aware that to develop eastern India agriculture was the key, not industry.

The seven sister states of north-eastern India, as well as the people of Assam, are also comfortable with farming. West Bengal, truly speaking, is also similar. Prior to independence, most industries in the state had been promoted by the British and very few by the indigenous people. When the British disinvested after 1947, not a single enterprise was bought by any local entrepreneur save one, namely Jardine Henderson, which was invested in by a Gujarati from Prayagraj (Uttar Pradesh). The rest went to entrepreneurs from Rajasthan.

This was not desirable. The reason was that there was a divide whereby the locals felt that outsiders were the owners while they had become workers. A few of them from a *zamindari* background went on to become trade union leaders rather than entrepreneurs. This unfortunate divide, instead of promoting more and better industries, actually destroyed industry in West

Bengal. A state which in 1947 was the paradise of industries went on to become their graveyard by 1977.

Bihar and Jharkhand, too, are primarily inclined towards farming. At the same time, most of the region is well fed with water, riverine or through rainfall. Shillong in Meghalaya, for instance, may be at an altitude, but Cherrapunji in the same state is quite nearby.

In spite of all these factors, no special emphasis has been laid on farming in the east. It is not realised in our country that industry is the employment of machines and not so much of men. Machines earn depreciation for the company whereas the cost of workers, on account of annual increments, keeps increasing. As a result, the focus of an efficient industrialist is oriented towards reducing the quantity of the workforce, even if this has to be done by automation. It is true that the indirect employment that comes in the wake of establishing a factory or industry, like the development of transport and communication, housing, hotels and ancillary industries is useful. Nevertheless, the investment required to employ one person directly is quite high.

In India's northeast, the current productivity of the land as compared to its actual potential is low. Assam, apart from the tea for which it is famous, also produces excellent silk. Rubber plantations are becoming popular commercially in Tripura. Arunachal Pradesh is ideal for horticulture and fruit orchards apart from rice, maize, millet, wheat, pulses, sugarcane, ginger and oilseeds. Plantation crops such as premium coffee, cardamoms and tea are grown in hilly areas of Nagaland, while Mizoram specialises in floriculture and horticulture, in which it has become an exporter as well. The state also has good potential for forestry, fisheries and sericulture. Climatic conditions in Meghalaya permit a large variety of horticulture crops including fruits, vegetables, flowers, spices, mushrooms and medicinal plants. Manipur's climate makes it well-suited for horticulture, especially rare and exotic medicinal plants and herbs. Sikkim is home to the cultivation of crops such as maize, millet, wheat, barley, oranges, tea and cardamoms. The state produces more cardamoms than any other Indian state and is home to the largest cultivated area of cardamom.

India's northeast is thus a zone of immense potential which has yet to be tapped.

Of Independence
and Partition

In 2022, India has entered its 75th year as an independent nation after colonial rule. But as our prime minister has also declared—August 14th which is our neighbour Pakistan's Independence Day—is one that will be remembered as Partition Horrors Remembrance Day. This human tragedy was set in motion by Muhammad Ali Jinnah formally on 23 March 1940, in the Muslim League's plenum on the eve of passing a resolution to divide India. Excerpts from Jinnah's speech the previous day make it evident that the Qaid-e-Azam was clear about what he was advocating.

"Muslims are not a minority; we are a nation", Jinnah claimed. He further said, "Hindus and Muslims are distinct and separate civilizations, deriving their inspiration from different sources of history. They have different epics. Very often the hero of one is a foe of the other and their victories and defeats overlap. To yoke together two such nations under a single state must lead to growing discontent and the final destruction of the fabric. The history of 1,200 years has failed to achieve unity; India was always divided into Hindu India and Muslim India. Therefore, Muslims must have their homeland, their territory and their state". For Jinnah and his League, this was inexorable logic.

Jinnah did not stop at mere rhetoric. To convince the British that the two communities could not coexist in one country, he unleashed the 16 August 1946 Direct Action Day in Calcutta. Riots erupted not only in Bengal but spread up to Bhagalpur in Bihar. For a man of the elite who wore only Saville Row suits, did not wear pyjamas or sherwanis before embracing Muslim politics, couldn't do a namaz and enjoyed pork, this was a complete U-turn. The Qaid's younger brother Ahmed Ali, who was my maternal grandfather's friend told my grandfather that the brothers were culturally Parsi, and ate and drank what they liked. The elder Jinnah had married a beautiful Parsi girl, Ruttie Petit.

A telling incident narrated by Pran Chopra (later the editor of *The Statesman*), as a reporter witnessing a Muslim League rally at Jalandhar in the campaigning during the 1945-46 elections reveals how Jinnah was the man of the moment for the country's Muslims. He could address gatherings only in English—the only other language he knew was his native Gujarati; certainly not Urdu. In the middle of his speech, the call for *azaan* (Muslim prayer) was sounded. While the crowd trooped off to pray, Jinnah sat down on a chair to smoke a cigar, resuming his speech after the crowd had returned. No one minded. For them, he was the messiah who would deliver them what they ardently wanted—freedom from Hindu domination after the British quit. Cigar-smoking and pork-eating were small details that didn't matter.

Jinnah, the highest paid barrister in the British Empire was a brilliant courtroom advocate. To him, the Muslim League and his Muslim followers were clients; his final fee was a place in the hall of fame in history as the founder of a new country for his community. The Muslim desire for a separate homeland existed before Jinnah, but he was its effective articulator, winning it for them after unleashing violence on Hindus and convincing the British of the imperative for Partition. Jinnah talked to the Muslims only in English as he did with all his clients, except Gujaratis. Unlike Jawaharlal Nehru, Jinnah did not offer the Governor-Generalship to Lord Mountbatten for a year or so, but kept it for himself.

In the minds of the League leaders, on the eve of Partition, it was clear that all or most Muslims of India's provinces must relocate to Pakistan. Through 1946 and early 1947, Jinnah and his senior colleagues demanded an exchange of population at Partition. His press appeal was published on 26 November 1946 on the front page of the *Dawn* which was still being published from Delhi. On 19 December the same year, Raja Ghazanfar Ali Khan stated in the *Dawn* that the population map of India must change. The League President of Punjab made a statement that such an exchange was good. The other leaders who publicly agreed were Sir Muhammad Ismail of Madras and Pir Ilahi Bux of Sind. They and others were of the view that if Hindus and Muslims could have coexisted, what was the need for Partition? Justice Gopal Das Khosla, ICS, and a member of the Punjab High Court also held that an exchange of population was an integral part of Partition.

This view wasn't confined to Jinnah and the leaders of the

Muslim League. India's first President, Dr Rajendra Prasad, propagated the same in his book *India Divided*. He proposed that Muslims in India and Hindus and Sikhs in Pakistan unable to migrate should be allowed to stay on with visas issued by New Delhi and Karachi. Qaid-e-Azam Jinnah had endorsed his proposal. But the Nehru regime, adamant on foisting a rootlessness that would later come to be called 'secularism', sold the falsehood that Partition was a 'territorial' division and not a religious one, the consequences of which India continues to battle even today.

Bengal

A century ago the Congress leader Gopal Krishna Gokhale had said: what Bengal thinks today, India will think tomorrow. What a flattering compliment to a state where I grew up and spent thirty-eight years! Even after Partition, West Bengal maintained its position among the Indian provinces. Then began an inflow of hapless refugees from East Bengal, renamed East Pakistan. Chief Minister Bidhan Roy was a capable, honest and visionary leader but Jawaharlal Nehru did not allow him to handle the inflow of refugees. Nehru wrote to him letter after letter. To quote from one:

> I have your letter of August 4th about the influx from East Bengal. I realise your difficulties and naturally we should do what we can to help you. But as I told you long ago there is no reasonable solution of the problem if there is a large influx from East Bengal. That is why I think that it was a very wrong thing for some of the Hindu leaders of East Bengal to come to West Bengal.

I have been quite certain right from the beginning that everything should be done to prevent Hindus in East Bengal from migrating to West Bengal. If that happened on a mass scale it would be a disaster of the first magnitude. Running away is never a solution to a problem. I think the Hindu leaders of East Bengal who have come away have done no service to their people. If, as you suggest, things have gone too far already, then naturally we shall all do what we can, but I shudder at the prospect and the magnitude of the human misery that will come in its train. To the last I shall try to check migration even if there is war.

This is a sample of double standards of the Nehru dynasty. When it came to Punjab, there were many more coming in bloody trains—many dead, and only some alive. At the time rumours were afloat that Master Tara Singh, the Sikh leader, had threatened Nehru that if he came in the way of the hapless Punjabi refugees, the PM might be killed. Otherwise, why was there one policy for Punjabis and another for Bengalis? Notwithstanding, Bengali Muslims were not leaving West Bengal in any significant numbers. Here, it was largely a one-way traffic.

That was the time when the Hindu Bengalis referred to their Muslim brethren as *becharas* to be pitied but not disapproved of even after they voted for Partition almost a hundred percent.

There was no spare farmland for the incoming peasants so they were sent to Dandakaranya (now in Madhya Pradesh), which had been cleared for them. The refugees had been used to much more fertile land and, therefore, most of them could not adjust to the stony forest land and they returned to

West Bengal's refugee camps. The result of overcrowding of Calcutta was unwelcome. Several of the streets like Park Street, which once reminded one of London, become unkempt and commonplace. Yet, Dr Bidhan Roy, the physician-cum-chief minister, battled on to develop West Bengal. He built the two cities of Kalyani and Durgapur to create space for new industries. His only fault was to be subservient to Nehru, but then he was not a grassroots politician.

Dr Roy was immediately followed by Congressman Prafulla Sen who was clean and honest. He lasted for three years till in 1967 the general elections were called. The Congress was replaced by a United Front Government headed by Ajoy Mukherjee, a former Congressman often referred to as the Gandhi of Bengal. Once when he got fed up with the recalcitrance of Jyoti Basu, the Deputy CM, and their communist ministers, Ajoy Babu sat on a dharna opposite his secretariat, the Writers Building.

West Bengal, for 33 years or more, had to suffer the time-old communist policy of keeping the people on the frontiers of poverty so that they do not rebel but, at the same time, do not get strong enough for organising a counter-revolution. The only unusual step they took was to make peace with the share croppers, who were partners with the land owners. This Red government declared that 'he who tilled the land shall be its owner'. West Bengal shifted to three crops a year, the yields went up and the tillers were far happier. West Bengal has become a farming-cum-trading state in place of India's number one industrial state it was in 1947.

Javed Akhtar

Janab Javed Akhtar has equated the RSS with the Taliban, a prominent wing of the Islamist forces standing against virtually the rest of the world. Actually, the RSS is a socio-cultural organisation which incidentally also runs many schools. No RSS swayamsevak is on record to have fired a single bullet. Some believe Akhtar is a communist but to me he has appeared to be a Left-Liberal. His statement has done untold damage to Indian Muslims.

In my eight-year endeavour to learn spoken Urdu, I have made several friends in Akhtar's community. In the last few years, many of them and their relatives and friends have begun to integrate themselves with the new Indian ethos which is to live as an equal Indian without appeasement. The Nehruvian ethos has passed and is being replaced by a Hindu era without being against any religion. Akhtar saheb's statement, quite unprovoked, has disturbed the switchover from what has passed to the new whose dawn has broken. A number of

Hindus who were helping integration may go back and say that even a communist Muslim is a Muslim first. The Muslim womenfolk are trying to break the shackles of the rules laid down by their religion.

Prima facie, it would appear that Islam and communism are sharply different. The Muslim lives by his religion all day while the Marxists deny God and call religion the opium of the masses. In the Soviet Union, most mosques were converted into shops, municipal offices or party hangouts. Many a youthful CPM member used to enjoy declaring that they were pure atheists, particularly on the floor of Parliament. But historically, in India the Muslim parties and the communists have been allies. The CPI (undivided in those days) not only supported the Partition of India but even splitting of the country into 16 nationalities, if need be. At the other end, when Sir Abdul Rahim and Fazlur Rahman were negotiating with a prominent Hindu leader for a united Bengal as a third dominion along with Pakistan and Hindustan, the CPI and Jinnah were enthusiastic supporters. This was Jinnah's way of gobbling up the whole of Bengal instead of only East Bengal. Whatever worked to cut up India, the CPI was at its service. Even after Janab Akhtar's faux pas, two communist leaders came to his support on television channels, in whatever little I saw and heard.

The secret behind this opportunist stance appears to be fundamentally the fear of the Hindus. In their perception, anyone else who comes to power—capitalist, socialist or communist—can be, after an effort, defeated in an election. The CPM in West Bengal and the Congress in many States are examples. But in their assessment, once a Hindu party gets into power, it would be difficult to dislodge. It would build up a Hindu vote bank and its numbers would be large, larger certainly than any other vote bank, whether working class or minority. Pakistan has no visible communist; even in Bangladesh, which had tall Leftist leaders like Maulana Bhashani and others, they have long since been wiped out.

To go back to Javed Akhtar, does he not realise that his community as a whole has nowhere to migrate and they would be reluctant to emigrate? Why then should leaders like him seek to provoke Hindus into animosity? Pakistan, which should have been their haven, began to close its gates on the morrow of Partition. Punjab took Punjabi Muslims from the east. Most other Muslims were diverted to Sindh, which is where nearly all Mohajirs have had to gather. Now there is no further space, though Balochistan is one place where there is no problem of space. But how many Indian Muslims would find it welcoming? Elsewhere in the world the gates are closing, if they have not already closed. What is their future but to integrate in India? Why does Akhtar sahib disturb the atmosphere? Remember, prior to the riots in north-east Delhi in Feb 2020, there had been no rioting for seven years or more. We should leave it at that.

The question that remains is what in Akhtar's mind could be the result of his lyrics, himself or his community? No mature person speaks in public loosely to harm anyone, certainly not himself. Javed sahab is, of course, a veteran and anyone who has met him would assess him to be not only mature but also wise. He is also a gentleman and, therefore, he must have said what he did about the RSS to tell off the Sangh to improve itself by giving up all thoughts of a Hindu Rashtra. He should have known that he is safer in such a Rashtra than in a Nehruvian polity where there was frequent communal rioting—to tell the Muslims that Hindus are dangerous, so you better support us because we are the only party which can protect you.

Dilip Kumar

Years ago, I had reached my uncle's residence near Ritz Hotel in Bombay a few minutes earlier than scheduled. There I met Dilip Kumar; my uncle promptly introduced me to him. The matinee idol courteously chatted with me for a while asking me what I did. I replied I was employed by a tea-tasting company in Calcutta. "What are your plans for further progress (he said *taraqqi*)? *Film career ka kabhi socha hai*?" I said I didn't have the aptitude. That wasn't for me to presume, he said, but for a movie director to assess.

Indeed, Dilip Kumar's own cine journey was a twist of destiny. Had fate in the form of Devika Rani not intervened in the tumultuous year of 1942, he might have continued in his family trade of fruit selling. The thespian describes the start of his journey into tinsel town in his eponymously titled *Dilip Kumar: The Substance and the Shadow*:

> One morning, I was waiting at Churchgate Station from where I was to take a local train to Dadar (central Bombay)

to meet somebody who had a business offer to make to me. It had something to do with wooden cots to be supplied to army cantonments. There, I spotted Dr Masani, a psychologist who knew me well since he was an acquaintance. I told him I was in search of a job and trying to do some business. He was going to Malad (a western suburb) to meet the owners of Bombay Talkies and said it would not be a bad idea if I went with him and met them. 'They may have a job for you,' he mentioned casually.

There was warm recognition from Devika Rani (already a big star and boss of Bombay Talkies), who offered me a seat and looked at me wonderingly while I waited to be introduced. When Dr Masani introduced me, she greeted me with a *namaste*, her gaze fixed on me as if she had a thought running in her mind about me. She asked me if I had sufficient knowledge of Urdu. I replied in the affirmative. I wondered what sort of a job she was going to give me since she was so keen to know about my proficiency in Urdu.

She turned to me and, with a beautiful smile, asked me the question that was to change the course of my life completely and unexpectedly. She asked me whether I would become an actor. I had no experience and knew nothing about the art. She asked: 'How experienced are you in your family's fruit trade?' I told her I was learning, and could not claim much experience. She then said: 'There you are. If you can take pains to learn about fruits and fruit cultivation you can surely take pains to learn the craft of film making and acting.

Dilip Kumar found it hard to believe that Devika Rani had offered him Rs 1,250 per month, thinking the amount was an annual offer. Upon telephoning her, she confirmed that Rs 1,250 was for a month and not a year. She thought he had great promise and the offer should be one he would accept gladly.

I watched Dilip Kumar's first film *Jwar Bhata* in 1945 at Calcutta's Jyoti Cinema. Since then in my years at Kolkata until 1981, I saw many of his films, especially after my marriage. I believe Dilip's rise to stardom came through essaying romantic emotions suppressed in youth when caste acted as an unbreakable barrier. In those days, one could not marry without one's parents, often even grandparents' sanction. Expression of human emotions was stronger because of the restrictions. Dilip's films would have weeping and tragedy, a catharsis of sorts for cinemagoers of those days. Few could portray emotions the way he did.

In my view, Talat Mahmood's voice suited Dilip Kumar the most. However, Talat, quite early in his career in the presence of music legend Naushad lit a cigarette; it was enough to infuriate Naushad's sense of seniority. He told Talat never to come again to his office. Talat didn't figure in any of Naushad's films afterwards.

During the 1965 war with Pakistan, an unfortunate shadow fell over Dilip Kumar. It was alleged a Pakistani spy had hidden in his house. Years later, he was awarded Pakistan's highest civilian award the Nishan-e-Imtiaz. His political career began in 1980 with his appointment as the Sheriff of Mumbai. He was elected to the Rajya Sabha by the Congress in 2000.

Dilip Kumar's stay in Parliament wasn't notable, though he continued campaigning in elections whenever invited by the Congress. Our paths crossed when campaigning for the 1999

Lok Sabha elections. Retired Chief Election Commissioner TN Seshan was the Congress candidate against the BJP's titan LK Advani for the Gandhinagar seat. I was present at the BJP office in Ahmedabad. The Congress' public meeting was held immediately adjacent to our office and we could witness the meeting from the first floor. We first heard Dilip Kumar asking all non-officials to "get off the stage". Next, he ordered a bulky gentleman trying to climb up to the stage to "get down". It was none other than Seshan. Those gathered laughed and clapped; but even Dilip Kumar's star power couldn't prevent Seshan from losing his election at Gandhinagar.

Kerala

As one would have read, 20,000 of the Covid workers of Kerala, including doctors, nurses and others, were being suddenly laid-off effective from October 2021. It is possible that they were informed earlier but we read the news on 30 September. This came as a shock in three ways: firstly Covid was not yet over and the third wave was feared before long. Secondly, to be suddenly laid-off after working on a dangerous mission for say, a year and a half sounded unkind. Thirdly, I found it difficult to believe as I have worked in that lovely state of Kerala.

There was then a tradition, unbreakable, of 'Good Morning' money of Rs 50. Cochin, especially the Willingdon Island, had significant cargo traffic. If an exporter engaged a porter for even a day or two, the porter was entitled to be paid Rs 50 thereafter every morning for saluting the exporter. He had to be paid the money in cash every day the men turned up. Otherwise, many port workers would surround the exporter's office and a *gherao* took place.

Once talking to a tea trader from Malabar I sought his advice for a suggested diversification in addition to tea. The Malabari's response was uncanny. In Kerala, there can be seven trade unions for every six workers! One of the most intelligent people in India, the Malayalis allowed very few industries to survive and allowed almost no new ones to come up. West Asian employment saved the Malayalis to an extent; apparently every urban street has at least three gold jewellery shops, shining if not dazzling. The explanation must lie in the Malayali's propensity to work very hard once he goes out of Kerala.

In Delhi, I have come across several Malayalis who work on three jobs in 24 hours. Seven to 9 am, they attend a typing assignment at a lawyer's office; 10 am to 6 pm is normal full-day employment. Then they work overnight as a telephone operator who is allowed to doze off, but is sensitive to the telephone bell, which is essential for a nursing home or a small hospital. This is an incredible paradox: the Malayali works incredibly hard away from home but is a lazy, cantankerous workman in Kerala.

Does the explanation lie in the communist virus? From "each according to his ability to each according to his need" was a slogan of Karl Marx. Every human being has an equal need, hence all must be paid an equal wage. With intelligent work should come recognition in terms of promotion to higher rank but the pay packet should be similar. The average worker or officer may then take the view—why work hard? Do the minimum and go home. In the Soviet Union, you could do so but not agitate. Outside the communist society, the Red trade unions were formed originally to bring down the capitalist order by continual demands, higher wages, and fewer hours of work whose corollary was the employment of more workers for the same quantum of work. A cigarette factory 16 kms from the Writers Building, the central secretariat of West Bengal, had 2,380 workers with 119 different designations when 800 or so workmen and ten designations were sufficient. The trade union was honest but unimaginably unreasonable. Today, West Bengal is a graveyard of industry. In British times, it was the paradise of factories. Perhaps, something similar bugs Kerala.

Communism, in fact, came to the state much earlier than Bengal where a United Front government was formed first in 1967. However, in Trivandrum, a Left Front government was dismissed in 1960 by Indira Gandhi as a Congress leader with the blessing of her father. Nevertheless, it can be said that the genes of these states lent their people to communism from much earlier! Less work and more pay, until they went to work outside their states.

There is no doubt that ideologies, whether religious or socio-political ones, do affect the ethics of the people who believe in them. The theory of Max Weber on the Protestant work ethics is famous. The Catholics are believed to be comparatively more easy-going than the Protestants. There is no doubt that communism finished the Russian civilization.

There is another fundamental of communism that keeps the people from working harder. The first is the theory of equal needs; the second is the complete neglect of productivity. Karl Marx and his followers took it for granted that the capitalist economy overproduced and wasted the excess of production on consumption. Therefore, there was a tendency amongst Marxists to take production for granted. The focus of the communist was on distribution, which made the leaders and their followers neglect productivity and concentrate on incomes and wages. Above all, employment of everyone available was their constant concern.

Vote-seeking politicians did correct the neglect of agriculture. West Bengal attended to land reforms when the Left Front came to power in 1977. But Josef Stalin onwards, right until 1991, farm produce was neglected in the Soviet Union. Collectivisation of farms made the peasants enemies of all farmers—big, medium and small.

Kerala does not produce many food crops. On proprietor-owned farms, spices, coconuts, rubber, etc. grow well. And, of course, plantation crops like tea and coffee. This was also because there was nothing like collectivisation in the state.

Democracy on the Rise

Aspersions are being cast in the media that democracy is on the decline. Only those ignorant of history can say so. Today Europe is, prima facie, democratic at least to the extent of holding elections. Pre-WWII there were mostly autocracies, for example, Germany, Italy and Spain. For most of the 19th century and earlier, democracy was an Anglo-Saxon monopoly. It was heralded by England in 1215 with the signing of the Magna Carta or Great Charter by King John at Runnymede in Surrey. All citizens obtained some concessions and it was the beginning of the rule of law. Most of the noblemen were present at the signing at Runnymede. It began the tradition of the enforcement of the rule of law, which became a big pillar of democracy. All are equal before the law and all are to be treated justly.

The English noblemen had virtually forced the King to sign the charter; else, his endeavour would have been to avoid signing. Who is normally willing to give up power? It promised simple measures like the Church being given full freedom and London city being free to levy the taxes it used to earlier. All merchants could leave and return to England without harassment or taxation. Mild and acceptable measures were the beginning of modern democracy.

From those early centuries to the end of World War II was a long era of autocracy in most parts of the universe. In Europe, usually religion provided the ideology and monarchs came and went. China was a centralised empire for 22 centuries, uninterrupted. India had Muslim monarchs or emperors and Europe was dominated by the Holy Roman Emperor backed by the Roman Catholic Church based in the Vatican. The Eastern Church was at the beck and call of the Russian Czars. Africa was waking up while South America was an island with local kings until Spain and Portugal conquered them. Where was democracy? It was in England and later Great Britain, with Canada, Australia and other colonies following when they became independent. It came to the USA after 1776.

England and its leaders usually thought about what is fair, whereas other cultures were guided by what is right as prescribed by their religion. Yet others were conveniently guided by what is possible by might or right. Had it been otherwise, King Henry VIII would not have survived on the throne after leaving the Vatican Church merely for annulling his marriage to Catherine of Aragon and marrying Anne Boleyn. The independent Church of England has, thereafter, followed what suited the interests of England, not the presumed wishes of God.

Germany tried democracy called the Weimar Republic between 1920 and 1931, but failed. By May 1945, Adolf

Hitler's regime was roundly defeated. Thereafter, Konrad Adenauer came to power with his Christian Democratic Party; a democratic government has ruled thereafter. France was ruled by Napoleon III until 1870 when he was defeated by Germany led by Chancellor Otto von Bismarck. Italy was not a democratic country until after 1945. Eastward onwards there were a variety of autocracies.

India has performed admirably, especially because we started in 1947 with a low rate of literacy. Incidentally, Nehru was a democrat, who kept winning all the elections until he lived. So did his daughter Indira Gandhi, who won in 1972 and 1980 and her son Rajiv Gandhi in 1985. Except for two years between 1977 and 1979, the dynasty ruled India. The great advantage of democracy is the synergy it produces. Freedom gives enthusiasm to people while compulsion, which often results from autocracy, semi-paralyses nations and civilisations. As Prime Minister Modi said, India was able to achieve 100 crore vaccinations within some months because it was everybody's effort—the results of synergy are amazing.

Another reason for success of our democracy is the very size of the country where civilians or soldiers attempting a takeover would find it extremely difficult to capture power and hold it. Additionally, the country is so diverse in the language and culture of the people that a unity amongst people to capture and retain power is difficult.

An autocracy usually survives when there is no alternative. In a reasonably well-functioning democracy, this is usually not a problem as a vacuum seldom occurs. The nature and temperament of the people is important. Here the credit must go to the Hindu faith which makes people believe in their karma. To an extent this makes the people individualistic and they seldom want to unite to knock out another group. This is unlike Islam, which prefers rule by *jamhuriyat* or consensus under a monarch. The contrast between India, Pakistan and Bangladesh tells the story of different temperaments. The contrast between Islamic countries and the rest of the world is interesting. Wherever there is monarchy, the people are happy if they are Muslims. The concept begins with the Caliph who is supposed to be the spiritual and temporal head of Sunni Islam. The world of Muslims is meant to be one or pan-Islamic.

Air India

The plight of Air India would not have dipped so low had advice given in a national daily in 1983 been followed. The company might have been government-owned but three or four, preferably six or seven or more financial institutions beginning with LIC, Unit Trust, IDBI and nationalised banks should have held Air India through shares. They would be entitled to dividends, if any. The company would have been a member of the stock exchanges as well as chambers of commerce. Their senior representatives would have attended the shareholders' meetings.

The premier airline was a business and it should have been run as such, not like a *zamindari*. The acting zamindar was usually a joint secretary of the Government of India. He might have been a perfect bureaucrat, but was likely to be wedded to the correct procedure and not oriented towards profit. He would have worried more about audits than about results. That is not how business is run. Companies owned and run by the government are euphemistically called "public sector" without the realisation that it is an appendix of state capitalism. Where was the public as an owner, either direct or indirect?

The joint secretary, being from a cadre, was obliged to upgrade passengers free of charge. I had once travelled to London by business class with my family. Many of the seats in the aircraft were filled at the last minute before departure, with odd persons with whom I did not enjoy travelling. Mind you, I am not a snob; I have brushed shoulders with all kinds in politics. These appeared to be mostly relatives or friends of trade union leaders who had to be obliged to maintain industrial peace. In government, one had to do so; any effort to solve any case of industrial tension needed the blessings of senior officers, if not the Board of Directors. For officers, it was prudent to maintain good relations with trade union leaders, if necessary with soft-peddling.

To travel with such people was irksome for us; for European travellers, it would be an anathema. If say, 20 percent shareholding was also sold to the public, it would appear in public perception to be a company like any another. Industrial action would then be easier to take. For years, Larsen & Toubro was 54 percent financial-institution held and yet it was run like a private company and gave decent returns to its shareholders. It was only when Reliance Industries bought out some shares from some of the financial institutions that the 54 percent came into public limelight.

Another set of contributors to the sickness of Air India were the VIPs and ministers, whose recommendations had to be accommodated. Whether the person was required or not, he or she generally had to be appointed. Whether they were qualified was rarely commented upon. People in government seldom appreciate that overheads can bring down companies. That is what made Air India a treasure house of too many employees, at least four times more than required.

VVIPs climbed even greater heights. As soon as UPA-I came to power in 2004, a minister took off to Europe and bought a large number of aircraft. He repeated his performance soon thereafter by flying to the USA to acquire Boeing aircraft for Air India. The earlier lot of Airbus planes were for Indian Airlines. To top up his exploits, he had both the airlines amalgamated. No questions were really asked nor answered. The cost of borrowing drove the final nail in the coffin.

The bitter Air India experience need not forever condemn public money being invested in industry. A simple reason being that India does not have a sizeable and sufficient number of industrialists to industrialise the economy. Any common trader is not a potential industrialist. Yes, India has a large trading class and small-to-medium industry runners, but setting up a large industry requires a broader vision, a modicum of integrity, the ability to complete the project rapidly before inflation overruns the cost, and ultimately the ability to manage a large industry.

For the size of our economy and the dimension of India's needs, there are not many candidates around. In the 'liberal' days of Indira Gandhi onwards, it was easy to borrow money from the bigger banks. Quite a few big impressive houses, apparently successful, owe more they own. That is alright when a substantial part of the debt is from one's own shareholders and not from banks. Hence, let the government play its part as an indirect shareholder in a reputable house. Additionally, invite, induce and attract foreign houses but not in consumer products.

Let the foreign company suggest what they would like to manufacture. Thereafter, the government can verify whether the particular product is required in India. If it is, let the foreign firm decide how much and what percentage it wishes to invest. Then a public issue could be launched. What does not get subscribed can be filled up by the institution or banks. If the foreign firms to feel secure request the institution to fill the gap between 51 percent and what it invests, say 15 or 17 percent, it should be done.

Triumph and Tragedy

Proximity induces apathy rather like familiarity breeds contempt. Countless people in Delhi must have visited Tughlakabad. Moreover, any number of tourists visit the Qutub Minar each year. But how many of them remember having seen the mosque next door—Quwwatul Islam? The story of this mosque is told on the tablet displayed on the spot by the Archaeological Survey of India. It is a story of how 27 temples were desecrated and how their rubble was used to build a mosque in their place. Most of these desecrations had a political (rather propagandist) purpose. It was to announce to the regional populace that the Raja was gone and the Sultan had taken over.

In those days there were no means of communication other than the beating of drums which could not reach very far beyond a village. On the other hand, a popular temple was a place of pilgrimage several times a year. The devotees would suddenly discover that the sanctum of their beloved *avatar* had been broken to pieces and rebuilt with something that, in their eyes, was devastatingly offensive. Most often the old stones and statues that earlier adorned the temple walls could be recognised, for they had been used in building the mosque.

There is no record or mention anywhere that the idol of the presiding deity of the temple was removed and handed over to the priest for taking it away to another temple. In fact, in many cases, there were gleeful references to how the idol was destroyed and its broken pieces were placed at the entrance of the mosque. This was so that they would be routinely stepped on by those who began visiting the mosque.

The desecration that stands out is the one situated in Mehrauli which, until about 700 years ago, was the centre of the great city. It is situated next to the famous Qutub Minar. The masjid was named after its builder, Qutubuddin Aibak, as Quwwatul Islam, which translated into English means the "Might of Islam". The name itself is arrogant and for a place of worship it is even more so.

This mosque was built at the citadel which came to be known as Qila-e-Rai Pithora. The construction began soon after the Second Battle of Tarain, 1191 AD, wherein Muhammad Ghauri defeated and killed Prithviraj Chauhan. It might be recalled that at the first battle of Tarain, it was Prithviraj who had defeated Ghauri but did not kill him and let him go.

Many centuries earlier, Alexander of Macedon had fought King Porus in 326 BC on the banks of Jhelum but was forced by Porus to accept a bitter stalemate and return home. It is said that Alexander made Porus his ally. Ghauri evidently had a killer instinct. Anyway, to kill or not to kill is the privilege of the victor.

The Quwwatul mosque was built from the rubble of 27 Hindu and Jain temples that were demolished. It is a monument of a people's humiliation. If it were not so, all the statues that have been used in constructing the mosque need not have been so blatantly displayed. Even after 800 years, they are as it were alive for the conquered. And not only for the conquered but for all their successors who would visit this mosque. Surely, it is un-Islamic to have anything to do with images. Portraits and statues are *haraam* and yet, Quwwatul Islam has displayed them with a certain crudeness. If Aibak had been even slightly considerate not just towards the conquered but even his own religion, he would have covered the statues with lime and sand.

However, when one reads what Sir Syed Ahmad Khan of Aligarh fame proudly wrote about this replacement of 27 temples, one's impression of Islam gets shaken. What he wrote is best read in his original words from his Urdu book, *Asrau's Sanadid*, translated by Prof Khaleeq Anjum, (published in 1990, Vol I):

> Quwwat al-Islam Masjid'd Din Sam alias Shihabu'd-Din Ghauri, conquered Delhi in AH 587 corresponding to AD 1191 corresponding to 1248 Bikarmi, this idol-house (of Rai Pithora) was converted into a mosque. The idol was taken out of the temple and some of the images sculptured on walls or doors or pillars were effaced completely; some were defaced. But the structure of the idol-house kept standing as before.

> Material from twenty-seven temples, which were worth five crore and forty lakh of *Dilwals*, were used in the mosque, and an inscription giving the date of conquest and his own name was installed on the eastern gate.

When Malwah and Ujjain were conquered by Sultan Shamsu'd-Din in AH 631 corresponding to AD 1233, then the idol-house of Mahakal was demolished and its idols as well as the statues of Raja Bikramajit were brought to Delhi and they were strewn in front of the door of the mosque.

The relish with which the founder of Aligarh Muslim University appears to have written this is indeed surprising. At that time, the capital of India was still at Calcutta. Had it been transferred to Delhi, his pleasure might have perhaps been greater. For, the Raisina Hill from where India governed was only a few miles from Mehrauli where this monument to India's humiliation still stands.

What is fundamentalism?

The widespread abuse of the word 'fundamentalism' began in the wake of the return of Ayatollah Khomeini to Iran. He and his followers were labelled fundamentalist as are all groups who have Islam as the basis of their ideology. In the process, they use religion for the pursuit of their politics. That may make them theocratic but not fundamentalists.

The concept of fundamentalism owes its origin to the United States of America in the years following the First World War. The theory of evolution by Charles Darwin had crossed the Atlantic and gained currency in the USA; many including the liberals among the priests began to appreciate its contention. His great work, *The Origin of Species by Means of Natural Selection, or The Preservation of Favoured Races in the Struggle for Life* had been published in England during 1859. A storm of controversy immediately arose over the book, reaching its height at Oxford in 1860 when a scientist called TH Huxley and Bishop Wilberforce fought a gun duel.

Its acceptance threatened to pull the carpet from under the Biblical doctrine of creation.

It was a challenge against religion by science. The Christian belief was that God created the world over six days and rested on the seventh.

In 1925, a teacher of science in Dayton, Tennessee, named John T Scopes was tried and fined a hundred dollars for teaching Darwin's theory of evolution. Fundamentalism, therefore, related to a dispute between Christian Conservatives and Liberals. The former were called fundamentalists by the latter. The Liberals had the proof of scientific discovery on their side. The only way the Conservatives could defend or conserve their viewpoint was in appeal to the fundamentals which were ordained by the Holy Book. It had nothing to do with Islam and even less with the votaries of Hindutva who are now being abused as fundamentalists by the so-called secularists.

The group around Smt Indira Gandhi, then India's Prime Minister, introduced the expression in 1984 to condemn Jarnail Singh Bhindranwale, a militant Sikh separatist figure who was later taken down in a military operation. Thereafter, the word began to be hurled at any and all associated with religion or religious activity. Until then, the favourite expression was communal. The self-styled secularists have no idea of the meaning but think that the best way to curse someone they consider communal is to call him or her a fundamentalist.

Conceptually speaking, a Muslim can be a fundamentalist. Anyone who denounces change but cannot argue against it on the basis of reason is vulnerable to the charge of being a fundamentalist because he takes shelter under what is written in the Holy Quran or the Hadith and abides by the fundamental or the original. The controversy over the validity of *talaq* pronounced on one occasion or spaced over three months is one between conservatives and liberals. The latter may call the former fundamentalists. So could be the case with those who oppose the grant of maintenance or alimony to a divorced wife, as in the case of (the late) Shah Bano, on the plea of what was fundamentally or originally ordained.

On the other hand, a Hindu cannot insist on a fundamental. Hinduism or the Sanatan Dharma is *anadi anant* or one without a beginning and without an end. It has no comprehensive code or final message or scripture; no single book and no manifesto. Nor does Hinduism have a founder or a last prophet. Hinduism does not offer any finality; it indicates the possible directions. It can, therefore, afford an openness and a readiness to be amended by one's experience or the advent of a new discovery. A living example was the abolition of untouchability at the exhortation of Mahatma Gandhi. The Hindu approach can, therefore, coexist with science. In the words of former President Dr Radhakrishnan, the unity of Hinduism is not one of an unchanging creed or a fixed deposit of doctrine, but is the unity of a continuously changing life. This attitude 'cannot deprive the present age of its right to inquire and sift evidence'.

Sanatan Dharma does not offer any original fundamental or final ordainment under which its believer can take shelter. The Hindu cannot, therefore, be called a fundamentalist.

Heritage Hushed Up

One night during the monsoon of 1991, the rain was so heavy that it washed away the wall that was concealing the frontage of the Bijamandal mosque raised by Aurangzeb in 1682. This unusual masjid is a centre of attraction in the district town of Vidisha situated some 40 km from Bhopal. The broken wall exposed so many Hindu idols that the Archaeological Survey of India (ASI) was left with no choice but to excavate. For three centuries, these idols were buried under a platform that was used as the hall of prayers conducted especially on the days of Eid. Fortunately, the district collector in 1991 happened to offer protection to the surveyors of the ASI who were otherwise reluctant to expose themselves to the wrath of the devout.

Rich treasures of sculpture were thus salvaged. Some of the statues were particularly splendid; some went up to a height of eight feet. The work of the archaeologists, however, did not last long. The ASI soon received instructions to stop further work. The officer of the ASI working on the excavation was transferred out as was the collector. Whether this had anything to do with the new HRD minister (1991-1994), who happened to be the leader of the self-styled secular lobby in Madhya Pradesh, is not known. Since then, the Bijamandal mosque is marking time with a great deal of sculpture hidden under its southern side.

Aurangzeb was the last of the iconoclasts who had a go at this edifice, which was then known as the Vijay Mandir from which the successor mosque was known as Bijamandal. He celebrated his visit by renaming Vidisha as Alamgirpur. Despite some excavations between 1971 and 1974, which clearly showed that Bijamandal was originally a temple, namaz at Eid time continued right until 1965 when Dr Dwarka Prasad Mishra's government banned worship in what was a protected monument. Dr Mishra earned the gratitude of most Vidishans and many others in Madhya Pradesh.

Sultan Bahadur Shah of Gujarat was the iconoclast preceding Aurangzeb. He captured Vidisha and the first thing he did was to desecrate the Vijay Mandir claiming that the conquest of Bhilsa (the earlier name of Vidisha) was in the service of Islam. The episode is recorded in *Mirat-i-Sikandri*. About 200 years earlier, Sultan Alauddin Khilji had also enjoyed the pleasure of damaging Vijay Mandir. The honour of being the first iconoclast, however, went to Sultan Shamsuddin Iltutmish, yet another century earlier. This episode is described in *Tabqat-i-Nasiri*.

Few temples in India have had the misfortune of having been desecrated four times. The ASI has yet to undo the damage by Aurangzeb. The work of excavation stopped some seven years ago is yet to be resumed. Admittedly, it is

Let Voting be Compulsory

In principle, there can be nothing objectionable to electoral vote banks. It is another name for a political base. Who can endure and flourish in electoral politics without a base? There is, however, a particular reason for the vote bank having become a dirty expression. It has converged on one community; moreover, in order to appease this community it appears there are no holds barred. Why?

Take the example of Gujarat which has 16 percent Adivasis, 10 percent Dalits and 9 percent Muslims. The Adivasis are concentrated in the south and east of the state and have four reserved Lok Sabha constituencies out of the state's total of 26. Yet, no great effort was ever made by the Congress to appease them. The Dalits and Muslims are scattered more or less across Gujarat; prima facie, they can play limited roles—less influential in some constituencies and more so in others. Yet, the expression vote bank politics is invariably applied to only Muslims.

The Congress might not have loved the Adivasis less, but it certainly loved the Muslims more. The proof was the manner in which the grand old party's hold over the Adivasis was lost during the 1991 general election. The reason was a build-up of resentment against the oppression by the local Muslims called *Tarakdas*, a local slang term for Turks. For example, some among the latter community are into the business of lending money; when the Adivasi could not return the loan, he had to give his daughter to become the lender's keep. It is pertinent to recall that in the 2002 riots, the Adivasi *talukas* of rural Baroda were badly affected by violence as a continuation of protest.

One reason for giving the Muslim voters undue importance was the Congress conviction that up to 90 percent of them voted solidly—in contrast to the average polling of 50 to 60 percent. Another factor was the conviction with which members of the community went to the polling booth. In contrast, quite often Dalits were reported to have been chased away before reaching a booth through threats or violence by opposition musclemen.

The idea of vote banks began as a result of Jawaharlal Nehru's political need. In 1946, he was made president of the Congress by Gandhi in order to ensure that he became prime minister. Fifteen out of the sixteen Pradesh (provincial) Congress Committees (PCCs) had supported Sardar Patel for the post while one had opted for Acharya Kripalani; none voted for Nehru. The latter had every reason to apprehend opposition from many party stalwarts, especially the nationalists like Sardar Patel, Purushottam Das Tandon, KM Munshi, VN Gadgil, Morarji Desai and SK Patil et al.

In order to counter-balance these and other party men, Nehru's response was to exploit and consolidate his pro-

Muslim image, apart from his government sponsoring reserved legislative seats for Adivasis and Dalits. The reservations tended to make the Nehruvian and post-Nehru Congressmen complacent about the Adivasi and Dalit vote. This is one explanation for the growth of the Bahujan Samaj Party (BSP) and Ms Mayawati. Since there was no reservation for Muslims, many parties, including the Congress, felt they had to nurse this minority. The euphemism for this kind of one-sided focus is vote bank politics.

But more importantly, the indifference of the Indian voter results in an enormous waste of money. Every year in January, the Election Commission conducts a summary revision of the electoral rolls across the country. The electoral rolls so amended must be printed. Every five years or on the eve of a likely election, the Commission conducts an intensive revision of the rolls. With so much money spent by the government, if half the people do not exercise their franchise, does it not make such a system only half a democracy?

Prime Minister Narendra Modi's proposal, voiced a couple of years ago, to make voting compulsory for everyone whose name appears on the electoral rolls would be looked upon by the Congress and allies with consternation. The factor of vote bank would virtually disappear when polling is nearly cent percent. A minority vote of about 1.5 percent then cannot clinch victory for a candidate. On the other hand, if in a particular constituency the polling is say, 50 percent, and one community puts in its full effort in voting, the favourite candidate will win. Apart from the distortion, imagine a 15 percent favourite would claim to represent all the people!

The way out of such a distortion is to make voting

compulsory. In Australia, it is incumbent on every citizen to exercise his franchise. If he fails to do so without a justification, he is asked to pay a fine of some 100 dollars. In our country, such a punishment for not voting may not be practicable. What is suggested is that anyone who fails to vote, without justification, should have his name deleted from the electoral rolls for a particular period during which he would not be able to use his Election Identity Card, which must be mandatory for making any application to a government department, whether to file an FIR or to apply for a passport.

Aurobindo's Life Divine

It was on 24 November 1926 at Pondicherry that Sri Aurobindo had his major vision of the divine which he called *siddhi*. Commenting on his greatness, the *Times Literary Supplement* wrote that: "He might prove to be one of the truly creative philosophers who have given a new thought and a new vision to mankind". The class of philosophers the journal had in mind included Plato, Kant, Hegel and Bergson. The same publication had elsewhere quoted Sir Francis Younghusband as having said that Sri Aurobindo's mystical magnum opus called *The Life Divine* was the greatest book which had been produced in his time (*Sri Aurobindo* by Peter Heehs, OUP 2005).

It is not widely realised that yoga means not only a union of body and mind but ultimately also of the human with the divine. True, the latter union is extremely rare. Over the last several centuries, only two individuals are reputed to have been able to view the divine, namely Sri Ramakrishna Paramhans and Sri Aurobindo. It is believed that both attained *mukti* (salvation); the former through *bhakti* (devotion) and the latter with the help of *jnana* (enlightenment) yoga. Their mystic experiences were at once similar and yet very different.

Sri Aurobindo was almost entirely educated in England over a period of fourteen years. In his second year at King's college, Cambridge, he completed his classical Tripos. Praising his essay on a comparison between Shakespeare and Milton written for the Tripos, Oscar Browning called it "wonderful". The famous poet went on to say that in his thirteen years as an examiner, he had not come across such excellent papers as this student's. Sri Aurobindo passed the Indian Civil Services (ICS) examination but ducked the appointment by missing the horse riding tests. Nevertheless, his learning was versatile ranging from the Greek classics to Latin not to forget Sanskrit and English poetry.

Politics and India's freedom had begun to stir Sri Aurobindo while in England. One of his biographers AB Purani has written that when he placed his foot on the soil of India at Apollo Bunder in Bombay, he experienced a tremendous peace. He proceeded straight to Baroda to take up his appointment which he had accepted from Maharajah Sayaji Rao before leaving England. He served the state for over thirteen years until he was 35. During those years, Sri Aurobindo took keen interest in politics in Bengal especially through his brother Barin. Being in the Maharajah's service, he had to remain in the background until the British government decided to prosecute him for writing in *Bande Matram*, a journal founded by Bipin Chandra Pal.

From 1904, Sri Aurobindo started practising yoga five to six hours daily. He called this practice *sadhana*. Although he did take a few advanced lessons from one yogi Vishnu Bhaskar Lele in 1907, the rest of his efforts all his life were his own. Incidentally, Sri Aurobindo attended the historic Surat Congress of 1907. Incredibly, he was already looked upon as a leading light of the extremists. Bal Gangadhar Tilak was his only senior. Although he had taken to political activity like a fish to water, it disturbed his *sadhana*. On many a day he could not even practise yoga; he found this disturbing.

In May 1908, Sri Aurobindo, along with some others was arrested in the Alipore Bomb Case. He left his defence to Chittaranjan Das and busied himself with *sadhana* in full view of the prison inmates. Once when the Governor visited the jail, he remarked that Sri Aurobindo's eyes were like those of a mad man. Charu Chandra Dutt corrected him by saying that they were those of a karma yogi! There were times when Sri Aurobindo experienced *siddhi*, the attainment of seeing light much greater than experienced in our world. At times, he was seen levitating, suspended several feet above the ground. On occasions, he heard the voice of Swami Vivekananda. During the trial in court, he saw Vasudeva and Narayana (forms of Vishnu) instead of the magistrate and the prosecutor. One day, in the course of a trance, he was reported to have experienced the divine. Aurobindo has written about how he was urgently removed to his solitary cell. In his own words, what happened then and day after day, he was not impelled to say except that "He showed me His wonders" (AB Purani). Thereafter, he often asked the divine for an *aadesh* or instruction.

After being acquitted in the Alipore Bomb Case, Aurobindo began editing journals called *Karamyogi* and *Dharma*. At the office one afternoon came an *aadesh* "Go to Chandernagore".

He obeyed immediately and reached the French colony the same evening. In less than two months, came yet another instruction which asked him to proceed to Pondicherry which he did on 31 March 1910 by a French boat named *Dupleix*. Despite a shortage of money, Aurobindo was able to concentrate on his *sadhana* while writing his epical poem *Savitri*.

His devotee, later the legendary Mother named Mira, wife of Paul Richard, first called on Sri Aurobindo on 29 March 1914, along with her husband who was a French journalist. She had repeatedly dreamt of Lord Krishna. When she met Aurobindo, she knew she had found the *avatar*. She had had mystical experiences since childhood. Soon, World War I drew her back to Europe. She could not return to Pondicherry until April 1920; this time never to leave until the end of her life in 1973. Her life was dedicated to the spread of the message of Aurobindo. Developing into a versatile organiser, she created the entire complex of institutions and the ashram.

Sri Aurobindo mingled more and more with the divine and found the ultimate success or *siddhi* on 24 November 1926. In his own words, life is all yoga. Moreover, his *sadhana* was not merely for his own self-realisation but also for the gain of mankind. After the attainment of *siddhi,* he confined himself to his apartment in the ashram and met no more than seven or eight outsiders in the course of the following 24 years. He was no organiser. It was the Mother who, in the celebration of Aurobindo, played the role reminiscent of Saints Peter and Paul for Jesus Christ or Ashoka in the spread of Buddhism.

Military: Defence in Depth

Victories in the recent cricket series have done a great deal for India's national morale. On most other fronts, we had not too long ago been on the defensive. Pakistani terrorists attacked Mumbai on 26 November 2008 and we were able to do little. On the economic front, there was a meltdown.

With growing competition, it is logical that coaches should begin insisting that their trainees bowl as well as bat. So far the approach has been to concentrate and consolidate the department of the game for which a youngster shows aptitude. Many years ago, there was little by way of systematic training from a young age; only a touch-up for adult players. Just as until many years ago, fielding in Indian cricket was taken for granted as incidental to playing, and not as a vital factor for being included in a team.

The next stage of evolution is for a bowler to be able to bowl with both arms. Since the beginning of the game, there have been ambidextrous cricketers. Some of them like Vinoo Mankad bowled with the left arm but batted with the right hand. Others did the opposite, like Sourav Ganguly who batted with his left hand and bowled with his right. Quite a few fielders can throw the ball to the wicket-keeper with either arm.

Different batsmen are vulnerable to different kinds of bowling; the greater, therefore, the variety in the attacking armoury, the brighter the chances of victory. Quite a bit also depends on the condition of the pitch. If everyone is coached and practises to be an ambidextrous bowler, there would be many more bowlers at the captain's disposal.

Going by the same logic, each batsman should be trained from childhood to bat with both hands, so that different situations can be countered with left or right-handed defence. For example, an outswinging delivery or a leg break by a right-arm bowler can be better defended by a left-handed batsman. If the suggested ambidextrousness could be introduced, a team of eleven heads would field 21 batsmen, 20 bowlers, 10 super fielders and a wicket-keeper, adding up to 52 versatile players.

The tooth-to-tail ratio concept was first observed in World War I. The British army had ten supporting men for every fighting soldier. The support included medicos, engineers, drivers and signallers. Since these men were not meant to engage in active combat, they were called the tail while the soldier with a rifle or a machine gun was known as the tooth. The German army's ratio during the same war was that for every tooth, there were only four in the tail which means the Germans were two-and-a-half times more efficient than the British. An average non-bowling fielder amounts to tail, not tooth, when his side is fielding. Similarly, a pure bowler is a part of the tail when his team is batting. In fact, he is called the tail even in cricket!

An old mindset about the batting order still lingers. This is that the better the batsman is, the earlier in the order he should be sent. The result is that the weaker batsmen often have to bat under pressure of time or score; they do not have the range of strokes required to score without reckless risk. It is, therefore, expedient to send the weaker ones early provided the innings has started well and there is no pressure. By the same token, in the event there are runs to score quickly or wickets to take to save the team from defeat, the quality batsmen should be more useful. In the military, this would be called defence in depth.

The approach to bowling also needs a change. As distinct from a Test match, a one-day international (ODI) does not require the bowler to be aggressive and go for dismissing the batsmen. Instead, the broad bowling strategy should be to bowl with immaculate accuracy and a good length on the middle stump reminiscent of Bapu Nadkarni who bowled maiden over after maiden over, often without taking any wicket. In an ODI, it is the batsmen who have to be in a hurry to score runs. Even if the bowler reduces his speed in order to achieve accuracy, there would be nothing lost. It is the batsmen who must hit out and hopefully get out.

So much so, that in an ODI, it is the bowling side which must be called the defence and the batsmen the attack. This is quite the opposite of Test matches wherein traditionally the bowlers are called the attack, whether spin or speed; and batsmen the defenders.

One great anomaly is that India with its 130 crore people is represented by an eleven-man team, whereas Australia,

Sri Lanka and West Indies, with much smaller populations, also have similar teams. Should not the five zones of India be allowed to play Tests and international ODIs, so that more Indian youth get an opportunity?